THE COMMONWEALTH:
A COMMON CULTURE?

For Shula,
with kindest wishes.
Peter
7. xii. 89.

THE COMMONWEALTH:
A COMMON CULTURE?

Essays by Professor Sir Shridath S Ramphal and others

Edited by
Richard Maltby and Peter Quartermaine

The University of Exeter for AMCAS
Exeter Studies in American
and Commonwealth Arts Number 2

First published 1989
by the University of Exeter
© *1989 University of Exeter and the several authors
each in respect of the paper contributed*

*Exeter Studies in American
and Commonwealth Arts*
General Editor: Richard Maltby

University of Exeter Press
Reed Hall
Streatham Drive
Exeter EX4 4QR

Typeset by Kestrel Data, Exeter

Printed in Great Britain by
Short Run Press Ltd, Exeter
ISBN 0 85989 318 9

In memory of Gamini Salgado

Contents

Acknowledgements

The Commonwealth: A Common Culture? records Sir Sonny Ramphal's unique contribution in 1986 to the academic life of the University of Exeter as Distinguished Visiting Professor, and his academic title (which he relished) is used throughout. Published here for the first time is Professor Ramphal's Public Lecture 'The Commonwealth and Common Purpose', a forcefully-argued view of the Commonwealth's role in a post-colonial world.

The other essays in this collection have a close bearing on Professor Ramphal's argument. In their range and variety they reflect the range and variety of the Commonwealth itself, and in both their point of view and their focus of interest they indicate the diversity of response possible to the question: 'does the Commonwealth share a common culture, and if so, in what does it reside?'. They also hint at the mutually reinforcing links between governmental and non-governmental Commonwealth and academic institutions such as the University of Exeter. We are grateful for the assistance we have received in preparing this volume from the Commonwealth Secretariat, and in particular from Clive Jordan and Peter Williams. Hilary Perraton has provided a valuable Afterword on the progress of the Commonwealth of Learning since Professor Ramphal's visit to Exeter, when he announced the appointment of a Commonwealth Expert Group on Distance Education chaired by Lord Briggs. Neither the Commonwealth Secretariat nor its officers should be held responsible for any failings in the book, which does not necessarily represent the views of the Commonwealth Secretariat.

Our thanks go to the Publications Committee of the University of Exeter for their support in producing this volume, and especially to Barbara Mennell. Tony Clayden, Head of Graphic Design, and George Webb, Head of Typography at Exeter College of Art and Design, have given us invaluable help in the layout and design of the book. Beryl Phillips, Patricia Dowse and Debbie Leonard typed the manuscript, and Bart Hallett and Chris Williams designed the book.

Our colleagues, Mick Gidley and Ron Tamplin, have discussed this project with us at every stage from its inception. Finally, our thanks to our students: more than anything else, exploring and debating with them what we mean when we talk of Commonwealth culture led us to ask the question which is this book's title.

Richard Maltby
Peter Quartermaine   *Exeter, January 1989*

Introduction

In an interview on the BBC Radio 'Today' programme for 14 March 1988 (Commonwealth Day), Professor Ramphal commented that 'there are people who will like the Commonwealth less and less as it looks less and less like empire'. The post-colonial Commonwealth can no longer be seen as being unequally 'united' by the historical legacy of empire, and the basis of any new-found consensus must be agreed, not simply assumed. Any unconsidered belief in the cultural unity of the Commonwealth, especially one emanating from Britain, requires particularly careful scrutiny, for the former centre of the empire is now neither assured of, nor entitled to, any centrality in a Commonwealth of diversity and equality.

If what was once seen as the centre no longer holds, does all notion of a common culture fall, or do shared political and cultural beliefs still remain? 'Culture' here embraces politico-economic, as well as artistic-creative, forces; the British Imperial institutions that Commonwealth countries have experienced range from Viceroys to 'The Vicar of Bray'.

The reformulation of Britain's role within the Commonwealth is, therefore, crucial to any sense of the Commonwealth's cultural community. In what sense, if any, is it true (as Mrs. Thatcher claimed in 1987 to Commonwealth Heads of Government in Vancouver) that a Commonwealth without Britain would be a contradiction in terms? Professor Ramphal sees this post-imperial process as causing more heartsearching in Britain than elsewhere, but as of equal consequence to all Commonwealth countries, since the legacy of British cultural authority (however regarded) is their one shared point of contact. The reconstruction of British culture, from colonization to cricket (always most political of games, as C.L.R. James and Mike Gatting have both demonstrated, the former with considerably more eloquence and tact), affects all involved. This is equally so for those British citizens of Commonwealth origin who today live uneasily in what their grandparents could (from afar) revere as the Mother Country, as for those Commonwealth citizens whose acceptance of the Commonwealth as a viable political institution is partly determined by the wish to continue cultural exchange with Britain. Any such cultural exchange will, though, increasingly be a dialogue, not a monologue with sycophantic chorus.

For Professor Ramphal, 'The Commonwealth represents the supremacy of community over otherness. It is the negation of both dominion and racism.' Such communal sense has tragically failed in the case of South Africa – a 'corner of Empire' found unworthy of Commonwealth status – which continues to haunt members, not least by underlining tensions between the Commonwealth's origins in dominion and its present intent of 'harmonizing differences, even contrariness, within a framework of community.' The ever-present and intractable issue of apartheid also demonstrates the complex and indissoluble links between 'politics' and other spheres of life, much as some academics and sporting figures profess their activities to be 'above' politics. The issue of South Africa has made long-dormant principles explicit in many fields of life, and has threatened to destroy the present Commonwealth. That it has not been allowed to do so is testimony to the value which its members place on the Commonwealth connection, and not least as a source of solidarity in the struggle to end apartheid. Professor Ramphal records that Commonwealth leaders not only 'feared what they saw beyond the brink. It was that they cared enough for what they would have left behind.'

The concept of Empire contained many contradictions, and their residues mark the Britain that Commonwealth leaders cared for as indelibly as they do any other Commonwealth country. In his essay Bernard Porter explores a central paradox between 'free trade' and imperial policy, which, he argues, 'may have lain at the root of Britain's long and continuing relative economic decline'. The 'remarkable comeback' of the ideology of the free market since 1979 has, he suggests, 'undermined the practical utility of the Commonwealth to Britain, and consequently left her free to drift away'; South Africaa has become more needed as a bastion of capitalist 'freedom' against communism than shunned as the object of criticism it represents for the rest of the Commonwealth.

Ken Parker suggests that, even today, the notion of Commonwealth consensus itself offers little comfort where the issue of South Africa is concerned. Britain's lone position of trusting the impetus of free trade to effect change in South Africa at best gives confused signals to any nation looking to her (rightly or wrongly) for leadership; at worst it seems to confirm her adherence to a 'Victorian' policy of high-minded selfishness.

The exploitation of materials and of labour underpinning the South African economy reflects an imperialism which justifies itself by cultural and racial prejudice of the most naked kind. For Britain, the imperial links with South Africa are strong and complex, as British responsiveness to certain cadences of South African 'reasonableness' (as earlier to that Battle-of-Britain-pilot Mr Ian Smith) reveals. Blood still runs thicker than water, and Britain's position is uniquely important and un-comfortable.

Professor Ramphal argues the advantages for all Commonwealth members of an institution dedicated to mutual assistance, and based on reciprocal respect. That South Africa can quote Amnesty International's condemnation of Human Rights abuses in Commonwealth countries certainly indicates the diversity of governmental systems within the Commonwealth today but, as Michael Thorpe argues, such abuses strike at the very concept of free nations linked by, and for, common wealth. For Britain, the role of paternal/maternal dispenser and validator of 'Commonwealth culture' (as defined in Britain) comes dangerously easily still. Ken Parker notes the absence of Britain herself, the invisible but always-assumed referent, from London's Commonwealth Institute exhibition. Alastair Niven warns of the potentially distorting effect that a Commonwealth Poetry Prize awarded from Britain (and for a time even funded by profits from South African mining) can have. Equally, 'Commonwealth' in the titles of academic research institutions can subtly reinforce the perception of the Commonwealth as 'other', just as the British so often refer to 'Europe' as quite separate from Britain. (So, for example, entry channels at Heathrow Airport are labelled 'EEC Pass-ports', 'British Passports' and 'Other Passports' with supreme disregard for logic and diplomacy alike.)

Britain's decision in 1973 to seek membership of the EEC was often cast in its opponents' rhetoric as a rejection of the Commonwealth, and to the extent that there has since been a gradual acceptance (most recently by the Labour Party) of Britain's attachment to Europe it has weaned British rhetoric from its imperialist vision of the Commonwealth as cultural protectorate. But the notion of Commonwealth culture as the subject of paternalist institutions administered from and by Britain has not yet been replaced (at least in Britain) by an acceptance of the diversity of multiculturalism. Indeed, acknowledgement of Europe has itself permitted the return of a revised cultural isolationist attitude. This attitude was confirmed by the Falklands War of 1982, as evidenced by the ease with which the embattled island rhetoric of the Second World War Ministry of Information surfaced (along with a motley cast including John of Gaunt, Sir Francis Drake, Nelson and 'Bomber' Harris) as if from out the azure waves. Equally revealing of a Little Englandism unwilling to acknowledge a history beyond these shores was the enthusiastic comment in 1982 by a British Member of Parliament that the Falkland Islanders were 'indistinguishable from our own people'. His meaning was only too clear.

Any shared culture within which the Commonwealth might demonstrate its facility for harmonizing must take account of the history of cultural interaction between Britain and its former colonies. That history, and its legacy, may be little more than a common reference point from which diversity is explored, but its most tangible expression is the English language itself. A common culture can, in one aspect, be seen as grounded in a shared language, and Maria Couto, Alastair Niven and Michael Thorpe all pursue the various literary manifestations of that common language. The Nigerian novelist Chinua Achebe observed in 1974 that he had 'always assumed that the Commonwealth of Nations was a great bonus for a writer'; equally, he has stressed that for him English is a language 'in full communion with its ancestral home, but altered to suit its new African surroundings'.[1]

'Literature in English' can no longer be equated with 'English Literature' (whose canon in any case normally includes American, Irish and Polish writers, and occasionally such writers as V.S. Naipaul, Salman Rushdie and Patrick White). But there remains an irony in what Ngugi wa Thiong'o has called the 'Imperialist heritage', of the language, less at the point of production than at that of consumption. Writers using English as the 'first language of international communication'[2] often address an Anglo-American literary market-place (itself hardly bereft of neo-colonialism) more directly than they address their own societies. As Michael Thorpe indicates, the English literary tradition has been enriched and extended by this enlargement, so that 'we are no longer confined, in this international literature, to the more or less sympathetic outsider's viewpoint', but we might also pause to consider to whom the 'we' in these sentences refers, and by whom it is defined. Ken Parker argues that "common purpose' has, in each successive stage, been modified, as well as modernized . . . to ensure that the dominant ideas through which that purpose is expressed are those of the metropolis', and it is not difficult to see how 'we' may perhaps continue to define 'ourselves' in terms too closely related to Ken Parker's 'unrepresented dominant', the stereotypes of the Great Colonialist Tradition. Such questions, however, do not justify 'the temptation to retreat into a cultural laager', which, as Michael Thorpe argues, 'is an easier option than one which confronts critical contradictions and diverging attitudes in a Commonwealth dialogue that might serve as an example to the wider world.'

Maria Couto quotes V.S. Naipaul's concise articulation of the issue:

'The problem is that one came to England with the same words as many English people but the meanings of many English words were quite different'. Her essay examines the different relationships two 'Indian' writers of different generations have to the divisions and diversities presented by their writing of Indian cultures using an English language marked, in the main, by its misperceptions of those cultures. Is the result merely a bastardization of both traditions and a fracturing of the self forced to function in 'the state of linguistic instability and cultural chaos', or is 'the supremacy of community' revealed by the ways in which their characters successfully inhabit not only what Naipaul calls 'the worlds I contained within myself', but also a language which 'isn't English as she is wrote and spoke'? Different in its derivations and cadences, G.V. Desani's language is kin to the 'nation language' Edward Brathwaite describes: both possess not only the common referent of the language of an alien, imposed culture, but similarly process its idioms to accommodate it to their own context.

These writers all recognise that literal as well as artistic environments shape the expression and the perception of a nation's culture, and both David Lowenthal and John MacKenzie explore that still largely un-mapped territory between geography and politics. What Professor Ramphal terms the 'agenda of anxiety' for the Commonwealth, committed as he sees it to 'influencing international society for the benefit of all mankind', also goes beyond the category of high politics to include the environment and its ecological condition. In exploring the successful transformation of conservation policies from 'an aristocratic imperial elite to that of a bourgeois nationalist, and often left-wing, group', John MacKenzie not only indicates how the conservation ideal 'became a source of international consultation and understanding', but also shows that the benefits it confers on some groups, including tourists, are on occasion provided at the expense 'of the dietary or territorial needs of other less favoured peoples, often the original owners of the land'. His argument provides a further example of the complexities and con-tradictions dormant in the idea of a common culture, in which 'One person's conservation can be another person's dispossession'.

David Lowenthal argues that the new small states of the Common-wealth 'exemplify the anti-imperialist ethos of self-determination . . . notwithstanding their evident frailties, and draw strength from a legacy that honours diversity and self-determination . . . a legacy they might well pass on to the rest of the world'. To that extent such states provide practical evidence of Professor Ramphal's vision of the Commonwealth as 'part keeper of the grail of internationalism'. However, such diversity is not only under constant threat from more metropolitan and monocultural values, but its mechanisms are difficult even for sympathetic outsiders to comprehend. It is even harder to see how such delicate and local mechanisms might be applied to larger entities held together, as Professor Ramphal himself suggests, 'by the intangible quality of a sense of togetherness . . . a relationship rooted more in intuition than in logic'.

Grappling with the admitted complexities of the Commonwealth's origins, nature, scope and potential – above all its multifarious traditions and talents – can lead us 'to understand our own history, not as something unitary, but as the story of different peoples and different cultures, a microcosm of the world which can help us to understand the rest of the world, as well as ourselves, a good deal better'.[3] Just such a modest but crucial commitment to understanding is to be valued as much in an academic as in a Commonwealth Secretary-General; where the two roles coincide, as they did at the University of Exeter on a day in November 1986, the fruits are greatly to be prized. In his Afterword, Hilary Perraton describes one such fruit in the progress towards establishing the Commonwealth of Learning. As he suggests, 'shared educational assumptions . . . are among the strongest links between the countries of the Commonwealth', and the Commonwealth of Learning represents a hopeful initiative towards a shared culture based on mutual understanding. The bases of such understanding lie in the past, but as Croce observed 'all history is contemporary history'; without that sense of urgency there may be no future.

NOTES

1. Chinua Achebe, 'The African Writer and the English Language' in *Morning Yet on Creation Day,* London, 1975, p.62.
2. Ngugi wa Thiong'o, *Decolonising the Mind,* London, 1986, pp.xi, 102.
3. Ann Dummett, *A Portrait of British Racism,* Manchester 1984 (first published Harmondsworth 1973), p.263.

I: SHRIDATH S. RAMPHAL

The Commonwealth and Common Purpose

Public Lecture by The Commonwealth Secretary-General
Sir Shridath S. Ramphal as Visiting Professor at the
University of Exeter 4 November, 1986

I am thrilled by the honour of being a Professor of this worthy University set in so choice a corner of England's garden. And it is not just the professorial status that thrills me. I looked in the direction of Exeter 40 years ago as a hopeful undergraduate before the antiquity (and the economics) of King's College, London, rooted me in the metropolis. The divinity that rules our ends determined – as ever, wisely – that there were some good things, like coming to Exeter, that should be reserved for me for later years. Even so, I must keep things in proportion. I am a Visiting Professor – here today, gone tomorrow. Tenure for one day; in graceful retirement the next. I shall not be able to write of 'a day in the life of a Professor'; but I can write of 'life as Professor for a day'. Were I to do so, it would be a sonnet of gratitude to Exeter.

You have asked me to talk of the Commonwealth. For that, too, I am grateful; since it is, in this country, in some minds, a time of questioning about the Commonwealth. That such doubts are not raised elsewhere in the Commonwealth offers a temptation to treat them here as a passing passion. But it was Britain's genius for political innovation that helped to give the world the modern Commonwealth. It would be specially disturbing if even a few in this country were to grow fainthearted about the common purpose which is at the heart of the Commonwealth's being. I know that the Commonwealth is vital and vigorous, and never more respected, both in and beyond its member states, than at present. I welcome the chance, therefore, to tell you why I believe this is so, and must remain so.

In conveying these thoughts and urging you to make them your conviction too, I have no wish to take you on a sentimental journey. I want, instead, to start with the present and not even with the Commonwealth. I want to invite you to share with me a vignette of our world and to explore together the validity, the legitimacy, the relevance of the Commonwealth's common purpose within that global environment. I want to ask you to imagine with me just what the Commonwealth can be in a world that shows signs of losing its way in the twilight of this fading century.

As I set out on that path I am acutely mindful that human reaction to the messenger hasn't changed much over the years. We have not come all that far from Phidipides at Marathon. As even the paragon of media virtue, the BBC, is finding out, the messenger is still at the mercy of his message. But messengers come in many guises and, today, the political process itself is at the heart of human communication on the state of the world. At that level, too, now as over the centuries, fear of the messenger's fate (which in democracies is loss of office) tends to give colour to the message that is carried by governments and that they would wish to have carried by others. And this, of course is true of governments everywhere. But this kind of universality only makes matters worse. It leads all too easily, I believe, to a false optimism, a philosophy of complacency, one that allows the advantaged, in particular, to pretend that our contemporary world is the best of all possible worlds – however abhorrent in reality may be the state of individual things, or the plight of others. Voltaire put it well, over 200 years ago, through Candide's revulsion over slavery and his renunciation of an optimism which he saw as no more than 'the mania of maintaining that all is good when all is bad'.

For the world community taken as a whole, it is close to the worst of times. As with those two cities of which Dickens told in his tale 130 years ago, it is also, I know, (in the minds of a few), close to the best of times. But those few are not in all respects more than the many; and it is of the many that I speak; the great majority of the world's 5 billion people, in poor countries and in rich.

For many of them the norm is life expectancy of less than 40 years, as in Sierra Leone or Guinea (compared with 75 in France or Japan); infant mortality rates in excess of 150 per thousand, as in Mali or Ethiopia (compared with 6 in Finland or 9 in Canada); per capita GNP of less than US$200 per year, as in Burma or Bangladesh (compared with US$16,000 per year in Switzerland or US$15,500 as in the United States). It is a world of extraordinary disparities between prosperity and poverty. But, even for the few who are advantaged, complacency itself is becoming a fragile thing.

It is a time, for example, which has produced greater unemployment in the industrialized world than at any time in the living memory of anyone under fifty; which has precipitated a debt problem of such staggering proportions that it threatens countries whose credit-worthiness has never been in question; which has seen commodity prices fall in real terms to their lowest levels since the thirties; which has produced foreign exchange deficits for the vast majority of developing countries so severe that they are depriving many an economy of even the capacity for survival; in which currency distortions have reached a state of 'mature anarchy'; in which protectionist sentiments have risen to such levels that they are becoming uncontainable even by governments for whom 'free trade' is part of the political credo.

And all this against a backdrop of nationalism that takes us back to the decade before 1939; of anti-internationalism that batters the structures of international co-operation built patiently, and with sacrifice, over the post-war era; of militarism that implies a recrudescence of power and authoritarianism in our global society; of arbitrariness and indifference to principle that erodes the foundations of world order, and of fanaticism that makes a virtue of extremism.

The agenda of anxiety is a long one and not all the items on it are in the category of high politics. It is a time of vanishing forests, of encroaching deserts; a time once more of famine and of refugees; a time of disappearing persons, and of new categories of the deprived like the phenomenon of street children. It is a time when, in our world, rain sometimes falls with an acidic content the equivalent of lemon juice. It is a time of Bhopal and Chernobyl. It is a time of drug abuse of the most frightening proportions and of the abuses of national and inter-national terrorism, sometimes even at the level of state action. It is a time of human hunger for peace in its deepest, most profound implications.

Confronted with such massive need and the mania, against which Candide rebelled, of maintaining that all is good when all is bad, must we not raise again the despairing cry of Camus: 'The absurd is born of this confrontation between the human need and the unreasonable silence of the world'. And, absurd, indeed, are the contradictions of our time.

In New York, last year, Willy Brandt, in receiving the Third World Prize for 1984, spoke for people everywhere when he said:

> . . . In all civilizations and cultures, in all religions of all socie-ties and continents, the right to live was considered something special . . . Therefore, it is unacceptable to the five billion people or to the 160 states, it is terrifying, that they should depend on their right to live on a small group of people in the(ir) capitals [of the super-powers]

At Reykjavik early in October, the verbal agreements that President Reagan and Mr. Gorbachev reached came close to a promise to release the world from nuclear thraldom. It would have been a monumental promise. All the fire-power expended in World War II amounted to something like 6 megatons. The world's current nuclear arsenal is the equivalent of 18,000 megatons – 3,000 World War IIs. A single US Trident submarine represents 24 megatons of destructive power – 4 World War IIs. For the two atomic bombs that changed the world in 1945, there exist today some 50,000 nuclear warheads.

Is the option of agreement gone? Each side says it remains. But we dare not be naive. Not everyone was disappointed by the retreat from agreement at Reykjavik. The military-industrial complexes on both sides came close to being routed. They were rescued, as they see it, by 'Star Wars', which (with supreme irony) became their 'shield' against disarmament. They are now re-grouping, probably on both sides; and they will be joined by other like-minded interests – including some in Europe. The challenge ahead is whether they will be allowed to resume their ascendancy. For the sake of all humanity, the people of all countries, this must not happen. The opportunities missed at Reykjavik must somehow be recalled.

Insecurity caused by super-power confrontation is in close and complex relationship with economic insecurity. Just as nuclear war and its consequences cannot be contained within the frontiers of the participants, so the economic consequences of the arms race and heightened East-West tensions have wide implications for all people. The Horsemen of the Apocalypse kill, indeed, with hunger as with sword, but today they acknowledge no frontiers, certainly none that insulate the Third World, which has disturbing parallels with the biblical 'fourth part of the earth' over which they were given dominion.

As Barbara Ward once memorably declared: 'We dare not forget the really poor, who are the great majority, because prosperity, like peace, is indivisible'. That link between prosperity and peace is even more integral; in truth, they are conjoined. In our first report: 'North-South: A Programme for Survival', the Brandt Commission put it starkly but simply: 'More arms do not make mankind safer, only poorer'. The next year the UN Governmental Expert Group on the relationship between disarmament and development concluded after three years of study that the world can either pursue the arms race or move consciously to a more sustainable international economic and political order; but that it cannot do both. There is a dynamic between development, disarmament and security which we ignore at our global peril.

But ignore it we often do. Our troubled world reveals a growing disparity in basic human needs, with a majority of people forced to walk the darkened road – encountering war, famine, disease and death as an almost daily consequence of their poverty. In most of the countries of Africa, Latin America and West Asia, living standards have continued to deteriorate – or, at best, to stagnate – for the fifth year in succession. No improvement is likely so long as we continue on the present path. Indeed, in sub-Saharan Africa, per capita incomes have been falling for over a decade. This alarming trend has recently accelerated and, between 1980 and 1986, per capita output declined by about 12 per cent. Low-income Africa is now poorer than in 1960, and the World Bank projects a further decline over the next decade.

Yet the rich industrialized countries of the North have still not been able to find a way of speaking and acting across the divide separating them from the impoverished South. Despite the impulses of the human spirit released by the Band Aid Appeal, there is an overwhelming need for the world to move away from charity and towards justice if there is to be a true response to the challenge of global poverty.

The conclusion is as inevitable as it is familiar. It is that unless deliberate international action can be taken, in a partnership forged between developing countries, the governments of industrialized countries, the commercial banks and the multilateral financial institutions, the world economy can expect to move towards instability, protectionism, stagnation, and widening poverty.

Much of the task lies, therefore, with governments – governments prepared to resist the temptations of isolationism and chauvinism; governments willing to rekindle the flame of internationalism and multilateral co-operation lit at San Francisco over 40 years ago; governments committed to the proper use of international organisations – enabling them to make their contribution towards building a new political and economic order in a deeply troubled world.

What are the prospects for negotiated reform? As we discern the twenty-first century in the twilight of the twentieth, shall we still be in what Alastair Buchan saw as the 'era of negotiations' succeeding the post-war era? Or shall we have passed beyond it – abandoning notions of democracy and consensus between states, and entering a more autocratic world, one in which world order yields place to a world ordered by the strong? If so, the next fourteen years will be very different from the last. We shall have entered a new era of global authoritarianism – taken another step backwards (as we did twice before this century) in the evolution of human society.

It is here that 'the unreasonable silence' of the world of which Camus despaired becomes so central to the prospects for the future. The challenge that multiculturalism now faces is, in reality, a questioning of the benefits of international co-operation. It is a questioning encouraged by many factors – some of them rooted in the experience of international co-operation in the post-war era. But it is also, in part, induced by the passage of time which has blurred human memory of how diminished international co-operation brought the world to economic disaster in the 1930s and to near self-destruction in the war that followed. The need for international co-operation 'to save succeeding generations from the scourge of war' seemed axiomatic as the United Nations Charter was agreed at San Francisco. Just forty years ago: how different it is today. In only double the time between the First and Second World Wars, we are witnessing a repudiation of the promise the world made to itself in 1945.

The quintessence of that promise was progress towards a world less susceptible to the usurpation of power on a global scale, less vulnerable to the imposition of one nation's will; one more hospitable to world order, more hostile to arbitrariness and compulsion. A world, in short, not permanently skewed, with the few always more than the many, the wronged forever wrong, the righteous never right, poverty in the midst of plenty, a life of crisis for most, a crisis of leisure for some; pursuits of peace through preparations for war; search for survival through enlarging our capacity for self-destruction.

How can our human society respond to these absurdities? What contributions can countries and people make in helping to move our world away from them? Is our need for bridges across so many human divides not desperate? What then would we say if some 50 countries from lands in the six continents and five oceans, including people of different races, languages and religions, displaying every stage of economic development and encompassing a rich variety of cultures, traditions and institutions, were to manage to come together, freely out of their diversity, and combine with common purpose – committed to influencing international society for the benefit of all mankind?

There was, indeed, a time – not so different from our own – when men of vision reached towards just such a co-mingling with common purpose of a sample of our human society. They failed, and the war that followed has erased the memory of their efforts. But we do well to remember them again. Founded in 1932 as an 'International Society to promote International Law and Order through the creation of an Equity Tribunal and an International Police Force', the New Commonwealth Society was concerned with a global Commonwealth of Nations in the broader sense. Its aim was to reconstitute and revitalize the League of Nations as an international authority 'possessing the power to alter the public law, and to enforce it'. It sought to enable the League, by increasing membership and powers, to undertake any action which, in the words of the League's Covenant, 'may be deemed wise and effective to safeguard the peace of nations'. There were 17 national sections – a coalition of countries in the making.

Lord Tweedsmuir was one of its Trustees, Harold Macmillan on the International Executive Committee and Winston Churchill President of the British Commonwealth Section. In 1934, it republished an exchange of open letters between Einstein and Freud called 'Why War?', originally printed under League of Nations auspices. Churchill's speech at a luncheon on 25 November, 1936 was published as one of the Society's booklets. It warned of the dangers of war, and was clearly in line with the Society's policy of strengthened international institutions to avert war. As late as 1957, Clement Attlee, in a Lecture in Memory of Lord David Davies who founded the New Commonwealth Society, restated the Society's complaints with the League of Nations in calling for 'Collective Security under the United Nations'. The Society was clearly in the vanguard of current international developments. It was a late response to the 'unreasonable silence of the world'.

In her 1984 Christmas broadcast, Her Majesty the Queen, speaking as Head of our own Commonwealth, made the point that 'One of the more encouraging developments since the war has been the birth of the Commonwealth'. So it has been; and in some measure our post-war Commonwealth shares some at least of the aspirations towards which those great men were reaching in the 1930s with their New Common-wealth of Nations. The identity of labels is not the vital factor – although it makes its own argument; and there were important differences of emphasis. What is most telling is the identity of the needs generated by developments in the 30s and developments today; and the similarity of outreach through a Commonwealth-style facility. In some measure at least the yearnings of the New Commonwealth Society of the 30s serve to confirm that the modern Commonwealth now fills a critical need – and might, indeed, be longed for had it not evolved. That evolution, as Her Majesty said, 'has been one of the more encouraging developments since the war'.

A year ago at Nassau, on the eve of the 40th anniversary of the founding of the United Nations and the start of the International Year of Peace, Commonwealth leaders spoke out even more pointedly in reinforcement of their common purpose – their commitment to inter-national peace and security and to internationalism itself: 'In the world of today and of tomorrow, (they said) international co-operation is not an option but a necessity'. And they continued:

> We warn that a return to narrow nationalisms, both economic and

political, in a climate of tension and confrontation between nations heightened by the nuclear arms race, invites again the dangers from which the world set out to rid itself at San Francisco in 1945.

'We commit ourselves and our nations to work tirelessly in the pursuit of a world marked not by disorder and the use of competitive power but one governed by the principles of collective international co-operation and respect for the rights of all nations and peoples as the necessary foundation for lasting peace and assured economic and social development.

Their Declaration on World Order was the single consensus statement of commitment on behalf of any sample of the international community to emerge that year. The message the Commonwealth sent to the UN was on the basis of absolute unanimity; and Commonwealth leaders in New York spoke to it with conviction and commitment.

In doing so, the Commonwealth was showing itself to be part keeper of the grail of internationalism – one of the world's custodians of the ethic of international co-operation. And there were ways in which Commonwealth leaders gave practical fulfilment to that commitment to co-operation in their Nassau conclusions on international economic issues; in their agreements on action in relation to small states; in relation to the economic situation in Africa; in relation to the management of technological change and the problems of youth unemployment; in strengthening our work on the role of women in development; and in reinforcing their faith in the Commonwealth Fund for Technical Co-operation through replenishment of its resources. In all these and other ways, Commonwealth leaders worked at Nassau, unnoticed for the greater part by journalists in search of controversy. But Commonwealth leaders knew they had worked well.

It bears repeating, therefore, what we are today: a community of 49 independent countries whose variety is now so great that it is a major element of the Commonwealth's strength, indeed, an element of its validity. That is a remarkable thing, because in the beginning there was, for some, kinship and likeness, but for the rest, and for a long time, unequal relations that bred a spirit of struggle not of co-operation. Yet out of it all has emerged a community of countries with members who play prominent roles in NATO on the one hand and the Non-Aligned Movement on the other; in OECD and the Group of 77; some of whom are rich and others very poor; some of whom are large and others very small; some of whom are strong in military and economic terms, others who are weak and vulnerable in almost every sense. But a community, nonetheless, held together by the intangible quality of a sense of togetherness. Not togetherness in alliance terms, or even in like-minded terms, but one which draws on history and habit, familiarity and shared endeavour: a relationship rooted more in intuition than in logic and sustained not by great expectations but modest achievements.

'A facility for harmonizing differences, even contrariness, within the framework of community' might be a functional definition of the Commonwealth. The emphasis, of course, is as much on the capacity to harmonize as it is on difference or contrariness. And it is that capacity for bridge-building, more than perhaps any other, that gives the Commonwealth a great potential for the future. The contrariness which is within the Commonwealth is contrariness that is within the world; a Commonwealth capacity for harmonization is a matter of consequence to the whole international community. In New Delhi, in 1983, Commonwealth leaders, in their Statement on International Economic Action, actually alluded to this capacity when talking of the 'Role of the Commonwealth':

> We have carefully considered [they said] how the Commonwealth can make a distinctive practical contribution to remove differences and misunderstandings. We believe we can be particularly effective when, as a representative group of developing and developed nations, we can speak with a common voice to the rest of the world. We have found a common voice on certain specific and immediate issues and we believe we can point the way forward on the more complex, longer-term questions.

The question is: are Commonwealth countries, Commonwealth governments, ready to take the further step towards action? I believe the world would welcome it; in many areas, a frustrated world community is actually looking to us for such a lead.

This perception of the Commonwealth beyond its membership as a world resource, a world asset, is relatively new; but it is almost inevitable, given the conjecture – not altogether fortuitous – between an evolving Commonwealth facility and global needs. Quite recently the President of the Federal Republic of Germany, Dr Richard von Weizsacker, on his State Visit to the United Kingdom, underlined the value which the world was placing on the Commonwealth when he said this:

> The Commonwealth is not against anyone. It is a source of common sense in a world where that quality is sadly lacking. It cannot negotiate on behalf of the world but it can caution the world and help it to negotiate. The more the Commonwealth preserves its coherence across the oceans and the continents, the better for all – including my own country.

Can the Commonwealth preserve its coherence across the oceans and the continents for the betterment of all the world? That is a great challenge; but it is more than a challenge. It is a duty: a Commonwealth duty to maintain its common purpose and to advance it in a troubled world

Recently, Commonwealth discords in relation to Southern Africa issues have raised questions in some minds as to the Commonwealth's capacity to fulfil that duty. I do not entertain those doubts. To some degree, it is true, the Commonwealth through these events was on trial – and, in some respects, still is. Its credibility was on trial; its integrity was on trial; its capacity to act above the level of the lowest common factor of response was on trial. It was on trial in the eyes of the people within its member countries and beyond its member states. It was on trial in the eyes of the victims of apartheid, the oppressed people of South Africa. It was on trial by every cynic who has abandoned belief that collective action is possible across the lines of colour and creed. It was a trial from which the Commonwealth could not shrink.

The Commonwealth represents the supremacy of community over otherness. It is the negation of both dominion and racism. Apartheid is the embodiment of both. Minority white domination is sustained by doctrines of racial superiority and systems designed to both reflect and entrench racial inequality. Apartheid is the very antithesis of the fundamental values of the Commonwealth and, as such, poses an inescapable challenge to governments and peoples throughout the Commonwealth. It is a direct affront to all the Commonwealth's non-white peoples and, rather specially, to neighbouring black Southern African states. But it is no less of an affront to decent people throughout the world regardless of colour; white people who resent what apartheid seeks to do through a racist philosophy that wrongly implicates them.

Throughout the countries of the Commonwealth, therefore, whether their majority populations are black, brown or white, or are themselves so multi-racial as to defy classification by colour, apartheid stirs deep passions. In the collectivity of the Commonwealth those passions are multiplied as apartheid is seen to challenge almost the most basic tenets of the Commonwealth. That is why in 1961 South Africa had to leave the Commonwealth. Apartheid was not compatible with Commonwealth membership. It cannot today be compatible with Commonwealth acquiescence. The Commonwealth's response to apartheid is not merely a Commonwealth position on a serious issue on the global agenda; it is a statement about the Commonwealth as well. In part, at least, what the Commonwealth has been saying and doing on apartheid has as much to do with the Commonwealth itself as with South Africa.

Over the last year, from the inconclusive search for consensus at Nassau in 1985, through the unique and historic role played by the Commonwealth Eminent Persons Group in pursuing the path of fundamental change by peaceful means and in clarifying the issues in terms which won the world's respect, down to the Review Meeting of Seven Commonwealth Leaders in London early in August of this year – from all this, the Commonwealth did not merely survive, it emerged with at least some new strengths.

It was strengthened because, at the end of the day, the overwhelming voice of the Commonwealth spoke out in a manner which made the Commonwealth credible not only in its member countries but in the world community; a voice which reached beyond a solitary division within the Commonwealth to a wider unity within the world Community. The Commonwealth today stands taller because of it. Years from now, at Commonwealth gatherings, other generations will look back upon that moment as one at which the Commonwealth faced a crucial test and passed it with distinction.

It is no small matter that Canada and the Caribbean, India and Australia, Zambia and Zimbabwe, could be so much of one mind, could be so confident in their resolve, so sure of the moral and political imperatives involved, as to stand shoulder to shoulder before the world. It is no minor achievement that they should continue to work, as they have done with success the past two months, to encourage that world to join in what will surely be in history's eyes one of the epic struggles for freedom in the end years of the century. There will always be some who demur. It is already the case, however, that the very most hindsight will allow them to say is (as Ian McLeod said later in relation to the *Observer* newspaper's strictures over Suez): 'You can be wrong by being right too soon'. That is a judgement the Commonwealth can live with.

And let us emphasise the elements that were positive even then. The fact that Sir Geoffrey Howe's account of his findings largely confirmed those of the EPG in the briefing Malcolm Fraser and General Obasanjo gave to the meeting was, in some measure, a coming together. So, too, was the unanimous conclusion of the seven leaders that there had not been adequate progress since Nassau. So, too, was the fact that there was no argument between them whether further economic measures should be applied against South Africa. London saw the end of a 'no sanctions' policy within the Commonwealth.

On 15 of the 17 paragraphs of the London Communique there was agreement between Britain and the others. Those paragraphs are important. They underlined, for example, the agreed Commonwealth resolve – agreed among all seven leaders – to pursue 'a common path towards fulfilment of our common purpose, namely, the dismantling of apartheid and the establishment of a non-racial and representative government in South Africa as a matter of compelling urgency'. And all seven leaders went further; they reaffirmed the seriousness of their resolve that should the action taken to date fail to produce the desired effect within a reasonable period, further effective measures will have to be considered.

And, beyond all this, all seven leaders went out of their way to renew their 'firm commitment to the future of the Commonwealth and to the objectives which have guided it over the years'. I believe that renewal of commitment is a real one. I saw Commonwealth leaders go to the brink and pull back from it. And it was not only that they feared what they saw beyond the brink. It was that they cared enough for what they would have left behind.

But, of course, the struggle to maintain the coherence of the Commonwealth across the oceans and the continents for the betterment of all is a continuous one; the evolution of events in Southern Africa at this very moment merely confirms the challenges that still lie ahead. In facing those challenges, however, the Commonwealth will draw strength from its coherence in innumerable other areas.

Within recent weeks, Commonwealth Law Ministers, Commonwealth lawyers generally, Commonwealth Finance Ministers, Commonwealth Health Ministers have met. The Commonwealth is at work on many fronts, and on many it is at work without discord or disputation. In Harare in August, Law Ministers agreed on innovative co-operative action between Commonwealth countries to follow across jurisdictions the proceeds of drug trafficking – a scheme which could be a model for international action. In St Lucia, Finance Ministers held what they felt was one of their best meetings – and not just in terms of ambience but of agreement over a broad range of analysis and action regarding major international economic issues. In Nassau two weeks ago, Health Ministers agreed to explore a truly imaginative programme of co-operation in health development.

Let us, therefore, not be faint-hearted in the face of some discords. The Commonwealth has emerged from them with enhanced integrity and standing among its member states and in the international community. It has emerged with confidence in itself that is neither brash nor vain, mindful of its weaknesses and imperfections, but certain of its strengths and of its ability to use them wisely in fulfilment of its highest aims. It is not going to please all of its constituents all of the time; it did not please President Amin when it spoke out against his horrors, or some Caribbean countries in its stand on Grenada; but a worse fate would befall it were it not to face up from time to time to the need to disagree; even – though, I hope, rarely – with a country whose own genius for political innovation made the Commonwealth itself possible.

Let me then conclude with the question that was implicit in the title I gave this lecture. Can a sense of common purpose make the Commonwealth worthy of the potential for service – to its member states and to all the world besides – with which history has endowed it? I have no doubt whatever that it can.

Its strength is its variety, which means that difference is within it. But because it brings both a sense of community and a facility for communication to those areas of difference, it is a facility for harmonizing them. But that is not all, or not enough. It is the quality of the harmonization that matters, and that is determined by the nature of the Commonwealth itself. It is the Commonwealth's intrinsic character which, in turn, sets the standards, the aims, the principles, the goals of the Commonwealth.

Whether we are looking to a world of greater equity in economic relations, or of greater tolerance in politics, with a better chance for peace and security, with political co-operation in innumerable fields; the Commonwealth can show a way forward. When we are trying to reflect in our international lives the understanding we can no longer escape that all the world is a neighbourhood and all its people are neighbours owing each other a duty of care, the Commonwealth is a facility which all the world badly needs. What can such a Commonwealth not do if its member countries become truly alive to its potential, care enough about giving it is farthest reach for good, use it as an instrument for enlarging both ambition for human betterment and its fulfilment?

The path we have travelled this last year has not been an easy one, and there are hazards ahead. But to have journeyed together should serve to renew our will, as it has strengthened our capacity, to travel to a farther goal. I invite you to share with me a vision of that journey and the promise it makes to a wider world. The world is beginning to count on that promise. We must not in the Commonwealth be the last to recognise the worth of what we have – lest, in error, we diminish it.

2: BERNARD PORTER

Wealth or Commonwealth? The History of a Paradox

The modern British empire was built on a contradiction. What that contradiction was will be made plain in a page or two. It explains nearly everything about the empire: its origins, its growth, its nature, its decline – especially its decline; and the attributes and some of the problems of its successor, the Commonwealth of Nations, today.

To discover the contradiction we need to go back to the early nineteenth century history of British capitalism, out of which modern imperialism, in a curious way, sprang. The curiosity derives from the fact, which is well known, that early nineteenth century British capitalism was supposed neither to sanction nor to need imperialism, which was regarded by its leading theoreticians (like Adam Smith) as a costly survival from less enlightened times. The anti-imperialism of early free market capitalism was central to it: a cardinal tenet of the faith of men like Richard Cobden, for example, who believed that the whole spirit and ultimately the material effect of his free trade movement was inimical to the establishment of one nation's authority over another. On the eve of free marketism's crucial domestic triumph in Britain, in January 1846, Cobden looked forward to the fruits of its wider extension in the world, which he held to be inevitable. 'I believe', he told his audience in Manchester, 'that the desire and the motive for large and mighty empires; for gigantic armies and great navies – for those materials which are used for the destruction of life and the desolation of the rewards of labour – will die away; and I believe that such things will cease to be necessary, or to be used, when man becomes one family, and freely exchanges the fruits of his labour with his brother man'. That was the vision that sustained him thereafter: of a world of interdependent yet entirely free nations, living together in prosperity, amity and concord, with only the historical memories of empires and imperialism to remind them of their more primitive past.

It was similar, of course, to liberal capitalism's other vision, of the ultimate *domestic* free market economy and polity. Both derived from the early political economists' belief in the universal beneficence of the system they advocated: its advantages not only to the urban industrial middle classes, which were obvious, but also to every other class in society once the manna shifting through the fingers of Adam Smith's famous 'invisible hand' had filtered down. This had political implications, as well as economic. The 'filter down' effect would increase everyone's prosperity. As they became more prosperous, people would also – naturally – grow more contented with their lot. This would make them less likely to rebel. The means, therefore, to prevent or curb rebellions would become less necessary; which meant the gradual withering away of the state in a political sense too. In the middle of the nineteenth century, unlike today, economic and political freedoms were regarded as indivisible; economic liberalism automatically gave rise to a condition of political liberalism, or even anarchy (in its truest sense), in which men and women regulated themselves in their relations with one another, and required only the very weakest of state apparatuses to lubricate what was essentially a self-powered, or free-wheeling, economic machine. The same applied to international relations. The great free world market which was Cobden's – and Britain's – fondest foreign policy ambition would render power politics superfluous. It followed that empires, which were an expression of power politics, were also superfluous, and must soon themselves wither away.

But of course the British empire did no such thing. Instead it grew and proliferated from the 1840s onwards, mainly in Asia, Africa and the South Seas, either by the outright annexation of territory to the British crown, or else, especially in the early stages, by what today have come to be called 'informal' means. To a free marketeer this was unsettling. There were – and are – three possible ways of looking at it. The first was to regard the imperialism of the later nineteenth century as part of a reaction against free trade. The second was to see it as a transitional step along the path to eventual free trade: necessary temporarily in order to secure customers who later would come to realise the advantages of the connection without needing to be secured. The third was to view imperialism as more intrinsic to British capitalism, and an expression of some fundamental tensions which lay at its heart. That, of course, was the Victorians' own least favourite solution. But it may take us to the root of the contradiction on which their empire was built.

The problem was not usually thought to arise in connection with the 'informal' portion of that empire, which was not recognised as such at the time. 'Informal' imperialism means the domination of one country by another by means short of overt annexation and administration: most typically through economic pressures from powerful customers or supplies or lenders of capital, sometimes *via* an intermediary native collaborating class. This notion has virtually no meaning to a free trade purist. Commercial transactions – so long as no artificial constraints are placed on them – can only be fair and free. The market sees to that, by setting the criteria for fairness. Consequently all contracts entered into between the buyers and sellers of goods, for example, or of financial services, or of (non-unionized) labour, are matters of reasonable choice on every side, and entirely free from the kinds of pressures which words like 'domination' and 'empire' imply. This was what justified the mid-Victorians' professions of anti-imperialism, which were genuine, and prevented them from seeing the quasi-imperial bonds under the free trade surface which tied so many of their customers to them. It was different when those bonds cut through the skin. That happened when 'colonies' which had been informally dominated by Britain came to be incorporated into the empire proper, either because they would not collaborate any more, or because a rival nation threatened to displace Britain as the power which dominated them. It was then that Britain sent soldiers to subdue and governors to administer them, and the contradiction became plain to all.

This happened on a wide scale during the 1880s and 1890s, and then again in the two or three years following the first world war, which were the periods of greatest expansion of the formal British empire in modern times. Usually the immediate stimulus and cause of any new annexation in one of these periods was political, but with a long-established economic motive underneath. The economic motive was always ambivalent, mainly because many economically-motivated people preferred to exert informal influence over the areas in which they had their economic interests rather than for Britain to march in and turn them into colonies: but this, of course, is where the political factor screwed things up. If British commercial and financial capitalists could have continued doing their business 'freely', without the Union Jack to back them, they would have done so: but they could not in situations where either the natives, or European rivals, refused to play ball. It was irritating and irrational that they should refuse to play ball, in a game – the free exchange across national boundaries of goods, money and services – which was so plainly beneficial to everyone who participated in it; but the last years of the century had shown that people – especially continental Europeans – could be sadly irrational at times. Britain kept control of her own reason by sticking with free trade, even in her newly-acquired colonies, when everyone about her was pushing up tariff barriers, and some of her own citizens were beginning to have doubts; but it would have been impossible for her, without immense damage to her interests, to remain' aloof from this other, political trend. So, although imperialism and free trade were supposed to be antagonistic principles, she was forced to resort to the one in order to safeguard the other; which was rather like eating meat in order to stay alive to be a vegetarian, and just as distasteful for some.

Of course it may have been inevitable. Free marketism's vision of a non-imperialist world was predicated, as we have seen, on the assumption that the market really did work to the benefit of everyone, which may well have been a fallacy that would have been bound to surface eventually, to the detriment or even the destruction of the system. If this is so, then it makes the contradiction which is the subject of this paper an even deeper one. Empire, the antithesis of free trade, was also the product of it: simply because free trade could not work without, somewhere along the line, the conditions for it needing to be imposed. As the poorer and less 'developed' countries of the world came to be more and more 'exploited' by western capitalist enterprise they naturally began resisting, which was bound to provoke stronger measures in order to keep them exploitable. In much the same way liberal capitalism on the domestic level may always metamorphose ultimately into illiberalism – what today is called the 'strong state' – simply because its natural evolution is not such as to endear it as ubiquitously as was once thought. That is as may be. Clearly there is no room to explore this theme here. But in any case it need not matter greatly to us. The important fact – whatever caused it – is that the peaceful and unfettered expansion of British trade and investment in the wider world in the nineteenth century very often gave rise to what at the time was considered to be its opposite. And this had implications which were of enormous significance thereafter: to the empire itself, to the British trade which was at the bottom of it; and arguably to the whole subsequent history and nature of the British state.

It created two main problems. The first was economic. The trouble with imperialism was that it cost. Britain in the nineteenth century did her best to ensure that as little as possible of that cost fell directly on the shoulders of her own taxpayers, by making it a firm principle of policy (almost her only one) that colonies should be 'self-supporting'. But that did not solve the difficulty. In the first place, there was no way the taxpayer could avoid some of the cost: of military and naval establishments, for example, which were strictly British, not colonial, but were only as large as they were – and growing larger – because of Britain's responsibilities overseas. Secondly, even that proportion of the cost which fell on the colonies could be regarded as a burden on British capitalism in the long run. In many colonies it was the capitalists who had to pay the lion's share of the taxes to pay for their administration, simply because it was only the capitalists who had sufficient disposable cash; or else their native customers, which came almost to the same thing. However the money was raised it came ultimately out of the pockets of individuals or companies which – in free market ideology – could have made better and more productive use of it than government; it was money wasted, and so a brake on Britain's rising prosperity, which in the end was the basis of her true strength. Again, this mirrored another and more familiar contradiction which is supposed to have beset the British domestic economy over the past hundred years: between the need for low taxation to enable capitalism to prosper, and for high state expenditure, on items like defence and social security, to enable it to survive.

This dichotomy may have lain at the root of Britain's long and still continuing relative economic decline. It affected her more than other industrial countries because she depended more on foreign trade than they. In a way it was rather bad luck. When Britain had originally pioneered the industrial revolution she had no significant rivals, and so a free commercial run in the world outside. By and large (of course there were exceptions) she could extend her markets to the far edges of the earth, without needing either to betray her non-interventionist principles, or to incur unacceptable costs thereby. That was when the broad pattern of her trade was established. By the later nineteenth century that pattern was vital to her prosperity and possibly her very existence, but was also coming under a variety of threats. To cope with those threats Britain had to betray her principles, and the ultimate interests of liberal capitalism, increasingly. From this dilemma there was no conceivable escape. This was the scale of one of the two main problems which arose from the contradiction of her situation as an imperial power.

The other problem was to do with ethos, and may have been even more serious. It derived from the fact that the commercial men in whose interests the empire was primarily acquired were not the sort of people who could run it, chiefly because they did not believe in 'running' other people in this way. Much the same reason lay behind the fact that the Victorian House of Commons, and Victorian cabinets even more, were far from representative of the middle classes who are supposed to have been their masters after 1832, but were made up largely of gentry and professionals: simply because the middle classes were far too busy doing what seemed natural and right to them – producing things – to want to waste their talents and energies on what their ideology told them was no better than a regrettable necessity. To a great extent this did not matter, because the gentry and professionals to whom they delegated power had imbued their values anyway. But this indoctrination was by no means complete. Martin Weiner has described the way in which residual anti- or non-capitalist values re-emerged in Britain in the second half of the nineteenth century, encouraged largely by the public schools (in themselves another contemporary 'contradiction': for who would have thought that one of the most successful products of a free educational market would have been something so subversive of the values of that market?), to the considerable detriment of the 'entre-preneurial ideal' in Britain, by contrast with Weiner's own United States. The creation and acquisition of wealth became less respected than, for example, landed status, or any of the other traditional qualities of the aristocratic class. That was in Britain. Outside, beyond the ken and consequently the sanction of the middle-class majority, the situation was worse.

In a way it made sense, if you had an empire, to have it ruled by the unproductive classes, because that way they stopped being merely an incubus. Besides, they liked doing it, and – especially after going through the public school mill – were good at it. But it was also dangerous because they could not be trusted. Hundreds of capitalists with interests in the colonies found this, to their cost. Governing colonies was in itself an interference in the free play of the market. It could have been done minimally, to limit the damage. But the governors had other ideas. They believed – most of them – that they had a higher duty towards their wards, beyond facilitating the exchange of goods and labour amongst them. Some of them even had their doubts as to whether facilitating exchange was in all circumstances desirable. One example was in Lord Lugard's pre-1914 Nigeria, where capitalism, in the shape of Sir William Lever's huge Liverpool-based soap manufactory, was actively ob-structed, and forced to seek a more sympathetic field for its enterprise in the Belgian Congo. Lever was stymied because of an idea that had grown up in the Colonial Office that native Nigerians should be encouraged to produce co-operatively, rather than be 'enslaved' – the word was sometimes used – to market forces. In India the British patrician class had a similarly low view of unrestrained exploitation. This was usually the case in those colonies which had the strongest colonial superstructures. They illustrate a pervasive trend which is often ignored today, of *anti*-capitalist imperialism in some parts of the empire. Elsewhere, of course, it was very different. Many colonies were quite ruthlessly exploited – or, by another way of looking at it, modernized – by capitalists. They were mostly the colonies over which the British

Colonial Office had least direct control. A good example of this is Southern Rhodesia (today Zimbabwe) whose administration was more or less given over to its exploiters, in the interests of economy. As a general rule, therefore, more formal imperialism meant less capitalist exploitation, and vice-versa. This was partly due to the fact that the formal imperialists themselves were imbued with a significantly different ethos from the informal ones.

At bottom, of course, it all boiled down to 'duty' and 'service', and all those other notions which are commonly associated with the old-fashioned dictum 'noblesse oblige'. Hopefully when the time has come for truly dispassionate histories of the British empire to be written, proper credit will be given for the sincerity – even if it was not always wisely directed – of this motive amongst thousands of the men who actually governed the colonies. The attachment of the best of them to the welfare of their subject was as great as the attachment of the best of the home-based British gentry to the welfare of their peasantry, and sometimes as beneficial (though of course the free marketeer would have to dispute this). It was this which cemented what at first sight might seem to be their unlikeliest alliance, right across class and political lines, with paternalistic socialists in the 1930s and 1940s, under the aegis (mainly) of Rita Hinden's Fabian Colonial Bureau. That alliance was largely responsible for the two most remarkable developments in the history of the British empire in the twentieth century (decolonization cannot be classed as remarkable, because it was inevitable): which were the Colonial Development and Welfare Acts of 1940 and 1945, and the Commonwealth.

Both went right against the free market capitalist grain. 'Welfare' is wrong because it uses money unproductively and discourages individual self-reliance. The Commonwealth is simply unnecessary. It could be harmful if it imposed obligations on members which were irrational in market terms, rather like European diplomatic alliances had done in the nineteenth century, which is why free trade Britain had struggled so hard to avoid them then. Ideally, individual men and women only needed to relate to one another as buyers and sellers – *via* what Carlyle once called the 'cash nexus' – in order to maximise profit and therefore happiness all round. Therein lay freedom, and – if it was done on a wide enough scale – true internationalism. No other international organisation could possibly be as extensive as this implied. Some less extensive ones might be tolerated, if they did not meddle in the market too much. That for many years was the position of the Commonwealth, despite various preferential commercial treaties amongst its partners, which still did not make much difference – and less, for example, than the EEC did when

Britain joined it – to the 'natural' pattern of her world trade. Free marketeers could never have much enthusiasm for the Commonwealth; but at this stage they could happily leave it be.

The enthusiasts in Britain were, mainly, antediluvian imperialists, romantics, humanitarians and Fabian socialists; people who in former times had positively welcomed the empire for what they believed to be its contribution to the good of mankind, or else wished at least to see its successor making up for the bad it had done. Most of them had few problems adjusting to their own loss of authority in the new grouping, which some of them saw as the logical culmination of all the best imperialists' (from Macaulay onwards) ideals and aims. An analogy often used was that of a family, whose 'children' had now achieved their majority and had to be accorded equality with their parents; an image which fitted in neatly, albeit patronisingly, with the strong thread of paternalism which this kind of commonwealthism had evolved from. In the 1950s and 1960s this warm beverage of ideals and sympathies flourished healthily in Britain, encouraged by a plethora of Commonwealth Institutions and Societies, continuing Commonwealth trade links, and a steady flow of university students from Commonwealth countries subsidised, without audible complaint (probably because they did not know about it), by British taxpayers.

That subsidy was one of the first casualties of the revolution that took place in British politics in 1979, when the ideology of the free market staged a remarkable comeback against a previous trend which the empire-Commonwealth itself had done much to establish. The way had been prepared for it by the dissolution of most of the empire in the twenty years after the war, and the fundamental dislocation of Britain's external trade which was one of the effects of Britain's adhesion to the European Economic community in 1973, both of which undermined the Commonwealth's practical utility to Britain, and consequently left her free to drift away. As she did so, the contradiction which had bedeviled her policy for at least a hundred years began to disappear. The old-fashioned paternalists returned home, tried to run things paternally there for a while, but in the end grew old and retired. They were not replaced: or at least, not in such numbers. Their spawning-grounds – the public schools – adapted to the new needs of the market, for what one of their headmasters in 1980 called 'pirates' instead of 'prefects', and began breeding more entrepreneurs to fill the gap left by the falling gubernatorial demand. America looked on, and approved. The House of Commons was transformed by an influx of marketing consultants and estate agents into something far closer to the nineteenth century's ideal (though 'ideal' seems a strange word to use in connection with estate agents) than the nineteenth century's own parliaments had been. Restraints on trade, especially trade unions, had their wings clipped or even amputated. Universities, hospitals, and other similarly 'unproductive' concerns were run down. Notable exceptions were made of the army, the police, and the security forces: which may have sown the seeds of another serious contradiction later on. (You can never avoid contradictions altogether). By these means, and others, what was called 'socialism' – a foreign virus, apparently – was to be 'squeezed out' of the British body politic; in order to create a new, vibrant 'enterprise society', harking back to Victorian times, but safeguarded now by a very un-Victorian security fence.

This was ominous for Britain's relations with the Commonwealth. The very word 'common' (implying 'shared') went down badly with individualists. It also enjoined toleration, which did not come easily to ideologues who were too convinced of the correctness of their own way of life and government to feel the need to condone ways which diverged too greatly from it. It was irrelevant to the two main priorities of foreign policy: which were to extend the area of 'freedom' in the world, and to take measures to defend it against the enemy outside. (The 'enemy within' was the concern of the paranoid paternalists in MI5). On one occasion the Commonwealth became a positive menace to those priorities. That was in the summer of 1986, when the Commonwealth games in Edinburgh were endangered and in the event gravely crippled by the withdrawal of whole contingents of athletes in reaction to the British government's refusal to impose effective trade sanctions on South Africa. Some critics read into that refusal a covert sympathy for the policy of apartheid, but that inference is not strictly necessary. South Africa's importance for Britain was that she was a bastion against communism; sanctions would both undermine her defences, and weaken the influence of the factor most likely to liberalize her: the free exchange of goods and services. That, of course, was a classic Cobdenite position. The wheel had turned full circle; though it had shed a spoke or two and taken on some iron cladding since Cobden's time.

What Cobden would have thought of all this is difficult to say. It might have disillusioned him. In a way the only thing that had made imperialism – in the broader of the two senses we have used it in – as tolerable as it was to its subjects or victims in the nineteenth and early twentieth centuries was the 'formality' of certain parts of it. That formality was, as we have seen, both a product of Britain's commercial and financial expansion in the world, and its antithesis. It served to protect, albeit imperfectly, the subjects of Britain's capitalist empire from the full repercussions of their new relationship with it, and by so doing gnawed away at the roots of capitalism, with deleterious long-term results. In the 1950s and 1960s, during the process that was called 'decolonisation', this formal side of the empire was dismantled. The Commonwealth was supposed to preserve some of its most beneficial features; but those who hoped so reckoned without the impact of the great British reaction of the following decades. With its old imperial contradiction now removed, British policy could get back firmly on to its former ideological rails. Thesis had given rise to antithesis, but then returned to the original thesis (though with added riders) once again. Market values ruled OK. International capitalists could get on with their proper work of 'developing' weaker economies, responsible to no one but their shareholders, and free from the misdirected sympathies of all those old colonial fogies who had not yet grasped the cold realities of life. All this might have been fine by Cobden. He was a man of mighty faith if so.

3: MARIA COUTO

Enigmatic Arrivals

I would like to begin with two propositions.[1]

This paper was read at a series of seminars in Indian Literature in English organised by the Centre of South Asian Studies at the School of Oriental and African Studies, London University, in 1987.

The first is from Rushdie's novel: 'What you are is forever who you were' says Saleem Sinai in the course of *Midnight's Children*.[2] His claim generates the idea of a self forever captive in lost time, and, in an important sense, belonging to another place. The second is from G. V. Desani: 'Things are. They are there,' says Desani's Mr Hatterr, in exasperated wistfulness. What he implies is that the world cannot pretend that he does not exist, that certain historical events did not take place, nor indeed, that the past is irrelevant in the description of present joys and traumas, in the search for and recovery of a self. Saleem and Hatterr travel long years. The recognitions and arrivals they finally achieve are enigmatic, because they represent a mental process, a coming to terms with history. The country and experience they seek and simultaneously define is life itself; not India, nor colonial India; not Britain nor her cultural empire, but a sum total of all these in terms of values that affect the condition of all men.

The idea implicit in the title of V.S. Naipaul's *The Enigma of Arrival*[3] provides the framework for my discussion of historical events and private experience, of a social community and internecine strife in *Midnight's Children* and *All About H. Hatterr*. The idea serves to illustrate the aesthetic developed by the novelists to reveal the spirit of man and the supremacy of community, the human community. Although Naipaul's novel is elegiac and desolate, altogether different from the world of fantasy, comedy and the picaresque created by Rushdie and Desani, yet he did create such a world himself in *A House For Mr Biswas*. The three writers embark on a similar journey and a quest which attempts to understand the 'who you were' of Saleem's claim in order to confront the 'what you are'. In *Finding the Centre* Naipaul discusses this process:

> Half a writer's work, though, is the discovery of his subject. And a
> problem for me was that my life had been varied, full of upheavals
> and moves: from my grandmother's Hindu house in the country,
> still close to the rituals and social ways of village India; to Port of
> Spain, the negro and G.I. life of its streets, the other, ordered life
> of my colonial English school, which was called Queen's Royal
> College; and then Oxford, London and the freelance's room at the
> BBC. Trying to make a beginning as a writer, I didn't know where
> to focus.[4] . . . I grew up with two ideas of history, almost two ideas
> of time . . . two ways of thinking about myself.[5]

The Enigma of Arrival describes a sudden moment of illumination when
Naipaul shed the fantasies his education had instilled in him, accepted
his colonial Hindu self, and freed himself to write:

> The ideas of the aesthetic movement of the end of the nineteenth
> century and the ideas of the aesthetic movement of Bloomsbury,
> ideas bred essentially out of empire, wealth and imperial security,
> had been transmitted to me in Trinidad. To be that kind of writer
> . . . I had to be false; I had to pretend to be other than I was, other
> than what a man of my background could be. Concealing my colonial
> – Hindu self below the writing personality, I did both my material
> and myself much damage. . . . With that knowledge (so hard before
> it was done, so easy and obvious afterwards), my curiosity grew fast.
> I did other work; and in this concrete way, out of work that came
> easily to me because it was so close to me, I defined myself, and
> saw that my subject was not my sensibility, my inward development,
> but the worlds I contained within myself, the worlds I lived in.[6]

Saleem Sinai, the hero of *Midnight's Children* is annihilated at the end;
Hatterr is disillusioned but not without hope. The enigma lies in the
fact that the worlds and homelands they seek and simultaneously
describe are imaginary yet concrete and tangible; it lies in the fact that
the selves they project are bound by irreversible events and yet part of
the process and flow of history.

A brief look at this history is useful: Macaulay's *Minute on Education*
which made English the official language in India in 1835 gave birth to
an English-wielding white collar class employed in administration, in
the railways and the lawcourts. Their language defines, at one level, the
'babu' world of Desani's novel. The process eventually created a
professional elite – the class of Saleem Sinai's grandfather, Aadam Aziz,
a doctor educated in Heidelberg. Desani's novel was published the year
after Independence and encapsulates the self questioning of a whole
layer of Indian society in the post colonial world. The generation gap

between Desani and Rushdie (Desani was born in 1909, Rushdie in 1947) illustrates the social change.

Born in Kenya, Desani interprets the heyday of the cultural connection when the upper middle class clearly opted for the Western way of life and all that this must have entailed by way of cultural reorientation. His writing is steeped in English literary allusions, and colonial values set within Indian religious traditions. For both Hatterr and Saleem links with England and the English language are central to their perception of themselves. So is the tie that binds Saleem to India, a country that is neither Hindu nor Muslim but home. Both feel betrayed when historical factors destroy the security they once enjoyed. The narrative in each case describes the journey in search of self resulting in a truer perception after confrontations with social reality.

They attempt to descend from the security of what is described in *Midnight's Children* as 'a hillock top world full of things, things, things'; a world ruled by conventions such as the cocktail hour. In Saleem's case the departure from this world is seen as a personal choice; Hatterr exercises no such choice: he is blackballed from the Club. Both membership of the Club and his exclusion from it are inextricably linked with his perception of himself and the world. In fact, the structure of Desani's Hindustaniwalla Hatterr is a colonial construct within the deepest historical perspective. The novel opens the way for direct confrontations and juxtapositions. He gives us the adventures of the colonial product Hatterr in encounters with sages who are often frauds but through whom the writer suggests the depth of tradition and its importance. The fact that the sages are connected with cities – Rangoon, Bombay, Delhi, Madras, Mogulsarai – draws attention to the culture of the metropolitan centres of empire to suggest that colonial values, superficially grafted on to a substratum of tradition, have bastardized both traditions, Indian and Western, particularly when the values of both traditions are shortchanged to serve immediate and material ends.

The cultural moorings of Saleem and Hatterr were fixed with the deliberate encouragement of the British rulers who over the years carefully nurtured a distinct culture of shared values conceived by a shared language. As products of this culture, they function with the shell of one language and exist in conditions of linguistic instability, a fact that Hatterr refers to again and again. Naipaul's Mr Biswas, who is, in a sense, Hatterr's other manifestation, personifies this instability as well. He finally 'arrives', however, at a deeper and more zestful comprehension of life's human wellsprings than does the narrator of *The Enigma of Arrival*.

Desani defines the state of linguistic instability and cultural chaos by

creating Hindustaniwalla Hatterr's history in his own terms. Hatterr
breaks up the King's English to make it his own tongue:

> The ABC of the book. A man's choice is conditioned by his past:
> his experience. That's true of words too . . . To one M.P. stands
> for a Member of Parliament. To another, it might mean major
> parasite. Depends on his experience. That's all why this book isn't
> English as she is wrote and spoke'[7]

The power of Desani's narrative is that it works both in the actual terms
of the story line and in the fundamental concerns that underlie much of
the apparent incoherence of Hatterr's conversations with the sages and
with his friend Banerrjee. These provide the philosophical and the real
underpinning of the tale. In a vast space that encloses charlatan and
sage, wealth and exploitation, honesty and hypocrisy, Hatterr moves
with courage and a sense of humour. At one point he is literally stripped
bare. Assumptions are undermined or destroyed; his experience allows
him to perceive himself in relation to all men.

Hatterr often refers to 'India' in his conversation with Banerrjee which
suggests the lost ideal he seeks. This is balanced by Banerrjee's parallel
references to Shakespearian truth and wisdom, to legal terms and the
recourse to justice which should provide relevance to 'life situations and
life encounters' yet only serve to exasperate Hatterr who is in the throes
of these life encounters! Hatterr's quest thus moves beyond the situation
of the English speaking Indian, or even that of the Indian writer writing
in English. It develops into a poignant search for a creative vision and
a view of the world. The very terms of definition are shot through with
the darkness of inevitability and the cavernous passages of pre-history:

> Biologically I'm fifty fifty of the species. One of my parents was an
> European, Christian by faith, merchant merman (seaman). From
> which part of the Continent? I wish I could tell you. The other was
> an Oriental, a Malay Peninsula-resident lady, a steady non-voyaging
> non-Christian human (no mermaid). From which part of the
> Peninsula? Couldn't tell you either.[8]

The 'merchant seaman' parentage is evocative of several layers of
cultural history, and relates Indo-British experience and culture to
colonial values and not to those of Western civilisation or to a specific
British tradition. Hatterr's fifty fifty personality becomes, in Saleem's
definition of himself, 'a half and halfer', 'neither this nor that.' Hatterr
thought he belonged, is shattered to find himself thrown out, begins to
'go Indian', is riddled with contradictions, and finally decides to
'continue like hell' just as a human being.

Saleem's quest takes off from and extends the scope of Hatterr's history. He rejects, in a sense, the Club from which Hatterr has been blackballed and which exists in *Midnight's Children* as the world of Methwold's Estate, where the new rulers ape Oxford drawls, learn about the cocktail hour and the correct diet of budgerigars. His mature years are spent striving to arrive at an understanding of his alter ego, Shiva, who inhabits the slum.

Hatterr uses what he calls his 'rigmarole English' with passionate precision to 'arrive', as it were, in the vehicle of least compromise. His experience is made to suggest that the repercussions of the cultural connection on India are boundless since it permeates Indian life in various manifestations. One of the most amusing is the sage, who meditates, clad in only a loincloth; and, to protect himself from the cold, wears a balaclava on his head. Such details, absurd, bizarre, but fundamentally part of the changing scene, of life's passing show, endow Desani's novel with its incomparable vigour and tragic sense. He illustrates both the strengths and inadequacies of the cultural connection by creating a language of dissonance to disclose simultaneously cause and effect, cultural integration and divided sensibility, affinity and incompatibility. The process stretches Hatterr's confused speech beyond conflicts of race, religion and language to encompass the human community.

In *The Enigma of Arrival* Naipaul comes to an England of the mind which exists only in his own perception.

> Cows and grass and trees; pretty country views – they existed all around me. Though I hadn't truly seen those views before or been through their midst, I felt I had always known them. . . . Here was an unchanging world.[9]

He then begins to look around him from the point of view of Jack, the Englishman, and his little cottage garden. He perceives the fallacy of his assumptions regarding 'an unchanging world'. The new angle of vision dispels the idyllic view of the English countryside and English cows acquired in Trinidad from, among other things, the pictures of cows on tins of condensed milk.

Naipaul is specially eloquent on man's relationship to his surroundings, on that harmony between man and nature whose lack he clearly felt as a child. In England he sees Jack who had created a special land for himself where 'as in a version of A Book of Hours he celebrated the seasons.' His own experience of 'garden' evoked colonial plantations, 'great flat fields of sugar cane for agriculture created by the power and wealth of industrial England'. Commenting on his narrator Naipaul says:

> he has not only to identify his personality, he has to identify his

own past. He comes from a colonial society where garden plantations have quite separate association from the ones they have in England where to cultivate your garden, to grow your flowers, prune your fruit trees – these have very lovely associations indicating another attitude to the land and to men or men's attitudes to themselves. . . . The problem is that one came to England with the same words as many English people but the meanings of many English words were quite different. One of the themes of the book is the redefinition of certain words.[10]

Hatterr looks for India with greater vigour and hope; Bannerrjee's promptings and affectionate advice, however, do not always light the way, and often deepen the contexts of illusion and reality. He does arrive finally and coherently in terms of the human condition. Unlike Naipaul, Desani transmutes and transcends tradition and the scientific spirit to arrive at fundamental comprehension:

I am not kicking. I am not complaining against Tyranny of Law. Every curse, every blessing, every justice, every injustice, every truth, every untruth, which is (or seems or feels so) is according to Law. . .

Maybe, damme, all humans . . . just like you say, come from one branched-off source: our granddad chimpanzee, our gorilla grandma, and the orang patriarch. O.K. and granted. But sans sense, primates, and progeny of puny primates! Why bite one another now, though your ancestors might have?[11]

His final cry is vibrant and vital, a life enhancing battle cry which compares well with Mr Biswas's resilience. Saleem, on the other hand, who starts out with greater confidence and greater hope in Independent India, is depleted of the will to live, or indeed to find himself within the larger context. Not for nothing is Padma exasperated by his history, which he relates in various stages from pre-history to urban society.

'At this rate', Padma complains, 'you'll be two hundred years old before you manage to tell about your birth . . . To me it's a crazy way of telling a life story . . . if you can't get to where your father met your mother'.[12]

She wills him to rush through those layers and come to terms with the now of her pickle making and the riots in Bombay.

When Saleem finally does arrive at long last it is only to lose her. At one point when she walks away from him he expresses his unutterable need of her and his arrival is expressed in his recognition of the vitality of Padma, both woman and Goddess, the lotus-eyed mother of mud and moisture:

How to dispense with Padma? . . . How to do without her paradoxical earthiness of spirit, which keeps my feet on the ground? . . .
whose return I had so earnestly desired . . . my Padma! who along
with the yaksa genii, who represent the sacred treasure of the earth,
and the sacred rivers, Ganga Yamuna Sarasvati, and the tree
goddesses, is one of the Guardians of Life, beguiling and comforting
mortal men while they pass through the dream-web of Maya. . .
Padma, the Lotus calyx, which grew out of Vishnu's navel, and from
which Brahma himself was born; Padma the Source, the mother of
Time![13]

Born in the modern city of Bombay, Rushdie recreates the vitality and
eclectic culture of urban India with reference to history from 1919 to
1975. Although the history of Saleem Sinai is violent, with accounts of
the Amritsar massacre, Partition, the Bangladesh war and the excesses
of the State of Emergency, Saleem, born in independent India, is a vastly
confident young man. Rushdie uses word patterns to suggest the vigour
and liveliness of folk culture, the pace and variety of urban life, the
mythology of Bombay films, the brash exuberance of affluence, with
violence simmering and on the boil. He introduces the Western reader
to a vocabulary expressing Indian experience that goes well beyond the
koi hai, tamasha and funtoosh of colonial times.

There are two important arrivals in the novel, that of Saleem
coming back to India where he feels he belongs, after time spent in
Pakistan and then fighting the war in Bangladesh, and the earlier arrival
of Saleem's grandfather Aadam Aziz, the Heidelberg educated doctor,
who had left Srinagar for Agra and who returns in old age to die in the
temple of Sankara in Srinagar.

Both are significant and enigmatic. Saleem returns to reclaim
India and appears to try to do it assuming his Muslim identity. His
days in the magician's ghetto in Section III roughly describes the
Muslim dominated slums in Old Delhi and the Turkman gate incident
during the Emergency. There is no future for him here, nor with Parvati
who is taken over by his rival Shiva. Nor is he able to marry Padma,
his old love. They are separated by milling crowds and Saleem is adrift
whereas Padma rushes on, and appears to know where she is going.
At his final meeting with Padma, she bars his way, in fact, turns him
out.

Both Rushdie and Desani suggest the importance of culture and
tradition. Their novels reveal the need to recognise that religion and
culture are closely intertwined in ancient cultures and civilizations like
that of India; that the full implication of secularization in such ancient
cultures needs to be understood; and that when the definition of

secularization narrow-mindedly rejects the culture of the past, it has disastrous consequences. Hence the frustrated and despairing return of Dr Aziz to the temple in Srinagar for it is he who epitomizes the rational, secular ideal and has been the first to dismiss religion as superstition. He is lucky to have a comprehension that allows him to return, even if disillusioned, to beginnings; they are not too far removed for him to have altogether forgotten them. For Saleem, thrice removed from his past, the return, if at all, is enigmatic, indeed tragic.

Desani's novel explores this idea with a broader and deeper comprehension of Hinduism. Whereas Rushdie's novel encloses the reader within a vibrant and zestful exploration of cosmopolitan Bombay – fast cars, suburban trains, ice cream parlours, Sunday morning film shows – familiar to those who know Bombay, Desani moves at street level – the railway station, the bus stop, the paan shop, fairs where the flotsam and jetsam of urban India congregate. He tries to suggest that a tradition has been lost while Rushdie's Bombay reveals the infusion of technology and industrialisation. Desani's prose is shot through with the consciousness of epics which were woven into the textures of millions of lives in every generation for thousands of years, the symbolic presence of the Himalayas and the Ganga that informed the consciousness of Indians fundamentally and spiritually.

Some of these ideas are captured in the presence of Padma in Rushdie's novel far better than in the character of Desani's Mr Banerrjee who has swallowed old meaning systems and new value patterns without quite digesting them. He has a Shakespeare quotation at the tip of his tongue to suit every contingency, to the exasperation of Hatterr who is the one 'in the spot'. Banerrjee's legal jargon, his attempts to find a legal loophole to solve all problems, illustrates Desani's satire at his best, good humouredly castigating the pragmatism of the Indian intermediary who survives in both worlds but embodies the values of neither. Hatterr comprehends the values of both worlds but gains admittance to neither.

Padma, though untarnished, as it were, by Western education participates in the vitality of urban industrial culture and brings into it her own vigourous response to life whether to the art of pickle making or that of love making. She has not been uprooted, nor corrupted and hence shares in the characteristics which have given India distinction through long ages. In *Finding the Centre*, Naipaul resolves the tensions of the 'fractured self' in an evocation of tradition which, though lost, is alive in the mind:

> Our sacred world – the sanctities that had been handed down to us

as children by our families, the sacred places of our childhood . . .
had vanished. Every generation now was to take us further away
from those sanctities. But we remade the world for ourselves; every
generation does that, as we found when we came together for the
death of this sister and felt the need to honour and remember.[14]

Desani, in particular, explores the need to remake the subjective world
of meaning systems and values. He suggests that if culture without
science, as in some aspects of our tradition, manifests itself in magic and
superstition-ridden forms of religion, science without culture results in
dehumanization, in regression into animal behaviour and in sophisti-
cation of means without ends. These ideas permeate the whole of
Desani's novel. Rushdie illustrates these dimensions in Section III, with
the Bangladesh war, the allegorical journey across the Sunderbans, and
the section in the magician's ghetto. He also suggests a pre-commercial
civilisation in Section I in the character of the boatman Tai in Srinagar.
Tai inhabits not a meaningless universe (as against Dr Aziz's rational
and scientific universe) but his own universe, which he creates in terms
of his own meaning systems and transforms into a universe rich in
significance and value.

Despite the verbal pyrotechnics of Desani's style, the irony of his art
and Hatterr's continuous reference to personal history, a glimmer of
profound human concern runs through the novel. There is certainly less
self absorption in Hatterr than in Saleem Sinai, or indeed in Naipaul's
tired narrator. Transposed to the Western cultural scene this difference
may be compared to the humanity that illuminates the literary display
in James Joyce and the lack of it in Nabokov's unquestionable artistry.
To Rushdie's credit it must be said that the concern is expressed through
the tenacious vitality of India as recreated in the novel, a vitality that
eludes Saleem. It is a vitality that Hatterr recognises and embodies.

NOTES

1. This paper was read at a series of seminars in Indian Literature in English organised
   by the Centre of South Asian Studies at the School of Oriental and African Studies,
   London University, in 1987.
2. Salman Rushdie, *Midnight's Children*, London, Jonathan Cape, 1981.
3. V. S. Naipaul, *The Enigma of Arrival*, New York, Viking, 1987.
4. V. S. Naipaul, *Finding The Centre*, London, Andre Deutsch, 1984, pp. 31–32.
5. *ibid*, pp. 58–59.
6. *The Enigma of Arrival*, p. 134.
7. *All About H. Hatterr*, p.16.
8. *ibid*, p.31.
9. *The Enigma of Arrival*, p.38.

10. Interview with Melvyn Bragg, *The South Bank Show*, London Weekend Television, 1987.
11. *All About H. Hatterr*, pp. 277–8.
12. *Midnight's Children*, p.39.
13. *ibid.* p. 149.
14. *The Enigma of Arrival*, p.318.

4: MICHAEL THORPE

How Much is Everything? English Language and Literature in the Developing Nations of the Commonwealth*

It would seem a vain task to seek to define a common culture among the diverse ethnic, political and religious systems that make up the Commonwealth mosaic. Investigating such issues as civil rights, religious ritual, or, more narrowly, the status of women, would alone be enough to expose radical differences. Even the Commonwealth nations' shared colonial past takes so many varying forms that it affords no serviceable generalizations. There is, however, a shared *medium* of culture, the English language, and it has become something of a cliché to affirm that the literatures of the Commonwealth form a rich Common Wealth:

> It's good that everything's gone, except their language, which is
> everything   ('North and South')

Obviously the St Lucian poet Derek Walcott's 'everything' is a studied hyperbole: he knows English remains the colonial language, using which many consider at best a shameful necessity. The English tongue holds its own now, often for pragmatic reasons, as a *lingua franca* in the countries Britain ruled, but it cannot be quickly forgotten that it was originally introduced as an instrument of imperial control – and of an imperious civilization:

> I said to Uncle Hilaal, 'We know what conquerors with written traditions who occupy a land belonging to a people of the oral tradition do. We know they impose upon them a law which makes it unlawful to think of themselves as human. The European colonists have done so'.

---

* The 'first peoples' of the white-ruled Dominions, Australia, Canada and New Zealand, fall outside this essay's scope: bound to remain ethnic minorities, still colonized, they face distinct problems of accommodation with the dominant culture.

So reflects Askar, the Somali novelist Nurrudin Farah's hero in *Maps*.[1] Language is bondage here, no valued bond; it would surely be natural reaction to wish to break it.

In years to come, the principal voices in Commonwealth written (as now in oral) literatures may increasingly be found in the indigenous languages and will become known in English through translation. The pressure on writers to turn from English to their native tongue is likely to grow. For example, in 1977 the Kenyan Ngugi wa Thiong'o turned from English to seek a new national audience through his own Gikuyu language. Ironically, this very act – writing 'in a language that will allow him to communicate effectively with peasants and workers in Africa'[2] – made Ngugi politically dangerous whereas his novels in English, widely read and praised internationally, had not bothered the government. His play, *Ngaahika Ndeenda (I Will Marry When I Want)*, was banned and he spent 1978 in prison; in 1980 printed Gikuyu versions of both the play and a novel, *Caitaani Mutharabaini, (Devil on the Cross)*, achieved record sales. Ngugi had clearly shown that it could be worthwhile to write for 'African audiences first',[2] translations into English and other African languages could follow. What Ngugi means by an *African* audience is highly significant: writing in English first is to address, in many ex-colonial countries (or 'neo-colonial', as Ngugi sees Kenya), a small and shrinking 'petit-bourgeois' élite; economically, such writing subsists upon an Anglo-American readership. Another example: in India, in Bangalore, a short story written in Kannada caused a riot among Muslims, while R.K. Narayan who, from nearby Mysore, makes his strongest impression in London and New York, was urbanely discussing his new novel on British TV (1986). India, though, with its joint national languages of Hindi and English, and with several major indigenous literatures read by many millions, is a special case; it does not confront the writer with such a radical choice as Ngugi's. However, in nearby Bangladesh a Government-inspired campaign to replace English with Bengali has been carried on since 1987 with much heat and confusion. Yet within India, throughout the South Pacific island nations (with 1200 dialects and sub-dialects), in many-tribed Nigeria and across Africa, between the Caribbean islands, English will remain the 'first language of international communication'[3] in which the peoples Britain colonized can communicate with each other, within as well as between nations.

In many Commonwealth countries until Independence and for some years beyond, both linguistic and literary education focussed upon English, not indigenous languages and literatures, tending to the formation of a common English culture. The anglophile novelist H. G. de Lissers could write, in *Twentieth Century Jamaica* (1913):

. . . the manners and customs of the country, insofar as they are civilized, approximate English manners and customs, the life of the country bears the indelible impress of English influences; the language is English, the sentiments of the people are more English than anything else, the religion is English, and Jamaicans are proud of their connections with the British Empire.[4]

Such attitudes were found unchanged among Jamaicans emigrating to Britain in the 1950s.[5] Inevitably, in such a cultural ambience, English assumed the standing of a classical literature, as it were: it was natural to quote English writers, imitate their poetic styles and adopt the novel form when, on the verge of Independence in the late fifties and early sixties a sudden burgeoning of young Commonwealth writers began to portray their own societies, past and present. The 'Imperialist heritage'[6] has an obvious duality, most deeply felt perhaps in the Caribbean, where many writers are of mixed blood. In an early poem, 'A Far Cry From Africa', Derek Walcott asks:

> I who am poisoned with the blood of both,
> Where shall I turn, divided to the vein?
> I who have cursed
> The drunken officer of British rule, how choose
> Between this Africa and the English tongue I love?[7]

In the Caribbean the humiliating institution of slavery, imposed in islands whose native population had been almost wiped out, exposed the transported African people to a total cultural imperialism. The Barbadian poet and historian Edward Kamau Brathwaite summarizes its effects:

> What our educational system did was to recognise and maintain the language of the conquistador – the language of the planter, the language of the official, the language of the Anglican preacher. It insisted that not only would English be spoken in the anglophone Caribbean, but that the educational system would carry the contours of the English heritage. Hence, . . . Shakespeare, George Eliot, Jane Austen – British literature and literary forms, the models which had very little to do, really, with the environment and the reality of non-Europe – were dominant in the Caribbean educational system . . . the people educated in this system came to know more, even today, about English kings and queens than they do about their own national heroes, our own slave rebels, the people who helped to build and destroy our society.[8]

It is this cultural and psychic deprivation Brathwaite set himself to counter in his poetic 'New World' trilogy, *The Arrivants: Rights of*

Passage, Islands, Masks (1967-9). In many passages of the poem he uses, not dialect, but what he calls 'nation language' – 'an English which is not the standard, imported, educated English, but that of the submerged, surrealist experience and sensibility, which has always been there and which is now increasingly coming to the surface and influencing the perception of contemporary Caribbean people'.[9] Brathwaite writes in both his native Barbadian and the Jamaican vernacular; his rhythms owe more to Negro jazz, blues and spirituals than to traditional English styles, especially the 'pentrametric model',[10] representing a deeper common culture of which oral examples survive, earthed by the shared oppression of slavery, going back to the 18th century. This example, from Andrew Salkey's long poem *Jamaica* aptly comments on our theme:

> Culture come when you buck up
> on you'self
> It start when you' body make shadow
> on the lan'
> an' you know say
> that you standin' up into mirror
> underneat' you.[11]

Salkey and Brathwaite belong to a generation whose English schooling in the 1930s so deeply indoctrinated the sensibility that it could come more naturally to a Caribbean child to write of snow than of hurricanes, for an African to write about winter than the harmattan.[12] *That* was no common culture. As Ngugi, who 'read English' at Makerere in Uganda, puts it, 'language and literature were taking us further and further from ourselves to other selves, from our world to other worlds'.[13] Today's post-colonial child will write, albeit still in English, of his native flora and fauna – and will probably begin reading his own writers, not with a struggle to memorize the abstract images of a wholly alien environment.

It was an inevitable phase of the developing Commonwealth literatures during the fifties and sixties that writers schooled in an anglocentric curriculum should have assimilated English literary rather than indigenous (oral) influences, but this did not, except in minor cases, result in mere imitation. 'The language is mine, not the tradition' wrote V. S. Naipaul: how, we may wonder, could it be otherwise? Yet Naipaul's has been a controversial case which well illustrates the uneasy ambivalence involved in taking advantage of the colonial cultural inheritance. Naipaul has not disguised the fact that he was relieved to escape from Trinidad through winning an Island Scholarship to Oxford when he was 19. His early novels and his travelogue *The Middle Passage*, satirize 'the squalor of the politics that came to Trinidad in 1946'[14] the year of internal self-government. The Barbadian novelist, George Lamming, condemned Naipaul as a colonial ashamed of his people's origins in 'the peasant sensibility' which, he asserted, 'Naipaul, with the diabolical help of Oxford University, has done a thorough job of wiping . . . out of his guts. His books can't move beyond a castrated satire'.[15] Yet a few years later, one finds Eric Williams, the Trinidadian nationalist historian and first Prime Minister, regretfully endorsing Naipaul's harsh portrayal of anglocentric West Indians as 'mimic men' in his novel of that title (1967).[16] Another fellow writer, himself indisputably a nationalist who does not doubt he belongs to a viable West Indies, E. K. Brathwaite, praises Naipaul's best-known novel, *A House for Mr Biswas* (1961) as 'the first [Caribbean] novel whose basic theme is not rootlessness and the search for social identity . . . whose central character is clearly defined and who is really trying to get in rather than get *out*'.[17] West Indian cultural conflicts are often loosely categorised in ethnic terms, especially in Trinidad where Indians and Blacks (of African descent) form roughly equal parts of the population, but no such simplifying opposition fits here, since not only is Lamming, Naipaul's severest critic, black, but Williams and Brathwaite also.

Lamming's virulent reaction against the early Naipaul can be understood as symptomatic of a period when the chief impetus of the new writers, in turning the colonial language to their own purposes, was to express the *distinct* quality and character of their emancipated nations and peoples (of this Lamming's *In the Castle of My Skin* (1953) is an outstanding example). Thus the young hero, previously quoted, of Nurrudin Farah's *Maps*, in studying his *Oxford English Reader*, sees how the imposed colonial tongue can be seized for an act of retaliation:

> The written metaphysics of a people is their 'civilization'. So read,
> read in the name of 'civilization', I thought to myself. And write,
> write down your history in the name of the same 'civilization'. 'This
> is a pen'. 'This is a nib'. 'This is a book'. Power![18]

Command of English, in the newly independent countries, meant pen-power. Mastering 'the language of the master'[19] was no longer simply a practical way of 'getting up' in a colonial society, but could now be pressed into the service of a post-colonial campaign to establish new social structures and new values. Though minds would no longer be colonized in the schools, the task of establishing psychic independence must be undertaken, and everywhere English was the one common, available medium. In Chinua Achebe's Nigeria, and in 'English' Africa as a whole, English could unify and was flexible enough to become the means of expressing many kinds of non-English experience:

> A national literature is one that takes the whole nation for its

province and has a realised or potential audience throughout its territory. In other words a literature that is written in the *national* language. An ethnic literature is one which is available only to one ethnic group within the nation. If you take Nigeria as an example, the national literature . . . is the literature written in English and the ethnic literatures are in Hausa, Ibo, Yoruba, Efik, Edo, Ijaw, etc. etc.[20]

To those who might object that writing in an alien tongue distorts one's vision Achebe answered, concluding his lecture at the University of Ghana:

. . .I feel that the English language will be able to carry the weight of my African experience. But it will have to be a new English, still in full communion with its ancestral home but altered to suit its new African surroundings.[21]

Achebe's attitude in 1964 was both pragmatic and creative. He and his generation throughout the Commonwealth led the way in emancipating the colonized people from mere imitation of 'standard' English usage and style.

Such writers are among the foremost in contemporary English Literature, which can now be regarded as an international, not an insular, phenomenon: V.S. Naipaul, George Lamming, Wilson Harris, Derek Walcott, Edward Kamau Brathwaite, Samuel Selvon, Raja Rao, Anita Desai, Nissim Ezekiel, Salman Rushdie, Chinua Achebe, Ngugi wa Thiong'o, Wole Soyinka, Zulfikar Ghose, Austin Clarke. Not only have they enriched and extended the language, these writers have immensely enlarged, and added human variety to, the subject-matter and themes traditional English literature had encompassed. This has enabled, without need of translation, direct insight into peoples, societies, ways of life which urgently need in a contracting, interdependent world, greater openness to each other. We are no longer confined, in this international literature, to the more or less sympathetic outsider's viewpoint:[22] Forster's and Kipling's India, Conrad's and Cary's Africa, have found new critical contexts beside the works of Narayan, Anand and Rushdie, Achebe, Ngugi and Soyinka. Achebe has written that Joyce Cary's *Mister Johnson* inspired him to create what he sees as corrective fiction from an African viewpoint – from which he has also attempted, in both fiction and criticism, to counter the malign influence of Conrad's 'Image of Africa' in *Heart of Darkness*.[23] Indians who have deplored the probability that Forster's Aziz, or the Godbole N. C. Chaudhuri dismisses as 'a clown' will be regarded as typical can now point to a substantial body of Indo-English fiction that speaks for them.

Such developments as I have outlined show that English language and literature have become, in the post-colonial climate, hardly less a battleground than politics. Without exaggeration Salman Rushdie could entitle an article on the Commonwealth literary efflorescent, 'The Empire Strikes Back'. It has been a cleansing warfare, on the whole, equalizing contemporary English literature with sturdily independent offshoots, and providing correctives to the insularity and racial stereotyping of traditional English literature.[24] It has, however, exacted a painful cost, for the writer practised in telling anti-colonial truths is too much the idealist to settle down as the praise-singer of his independent nation. I have already quoted Naipaul's case as showing how, even from the earliest years of Independence, the native writer could become his new society's harshest critic. Many more would become anatomists of quickly developing internal ailments caused by tribalism, greed, corruption and governmental breakdown. Wole Soyinka chose to warn against *hubris* in the very play, *A Dance of the Forests,* he was commissioned to write for the Nigerian Independence celebrations (1960); by 1966 Achebe's prophetic novel, *A Man of the People* would expose the corrupt politics that led to a military coup in January 1966 and to Civil War; Ayi Kwei Armah's *The Beautiful Ones Are Not Yet Born* (1968) satirises the corrupted African Socialism of Nkrumah's Ghana; Ngugi wa Thiong'o, a bitter critic of British colonialism in his early novels, in *Petals of Blood* (1977) published a polemical novel depicting a chaotic breakdown of values in the Kenya created by another hero of the freedom struggle, Jomo Kenyatta. These African examples could be extended into a depressingly long list, to which many others could be added from Asia and the Caribbean.[25] At first sight, the common ground shared by this literature of disenchantment discourages hope of meaningful unity, but what value can there be in trumpeting a 'common culture' based on self-praise and self-deception? Official Commonwealth relations between Britain and her ex-colonies are often characterised by glib assertions of unity that mask fundamental contradictions. Throughout Africa, for example, the parliamentary system of government adopted at Independence scarcely exists in democratic form, but as an empty figment where one-party tyrannies rule and opposition parties are abolished or neutralized. Military rule, African Socialism, personality cults: their leaders meet at a conference table with representatives of the Western democracies and, chary of denouncing each other, agree to condemn South Africa for racism and injustice. There is nothing new in international politics of the double standard, but to make higher claims for the Commonwealth is to find a common bond, ironically, in English hypocrisy.

Yet as the critical works I have mentioned illustrate, there is a deeper bond in a tradition of social conscience and dissent which is one of the glories of English literature, from Milton and Swift, to Byron and Shelley, Dickens, the major Great War poets and George Orwell. It is a matter of influence as well as affinity. In Naipaul's *A House for Mr Biswas* the hero, isolated in a Trinidadian world which, like Victorian England, bears harshly on the aspiring individual, finds 'solace' in Dickens. As Doris Lessing who, as a dissident young white Rhodesian, found similar support herself, has pointed out, the 'awakening' of intelligent people in the colonies was 'very often fed by the generous age of British literature – poets like Shelley and Byron and Burns, writers like Dickens'.[26] Mulk Raj Anand's reforming novels, *Coolie* (1933) and *Untouchable* (1935), written during the Raj but directed against traditional *Indian* inequalities, were confessedly inspired by 'European Hellenism and its ideals of individual worth'.[27] The poetry of Derek Walcott, whose words give this essay its title, is thronged with echoes of an allusion to such English poets as Shakespeare, Donne, Marvell, Blake and Wordsworth – whose *The Prelude* Walcott's long auto-biographical poem, *Another Life*, resembles in shape: interweaving the growth of the poet's mind with a searching, conscientious critique of his evolving Caribbean world, during and after Empire.

Outstanding among those Commonwealth writers who have accepted, with all its risks, the role – strong in the English tradition – of the writer as outspoken critic of the political and social condition is Wole Soyinka, in 1986 the first African winner of the Nobel Prize for Literature. In 1967, before his imprisonment by the Federal Government during the Nigerian Civil War, he wrote:

> ...the European intermittent exercises in genocide have been duplicated on the African continent admittedly on a lower scale but only because of the temporary lack in scientific organisation. We whose humanity the poets celebrated before the proof . . . are now being forced by disasters, not foresight to a reconsideration of our relationship to the outer world . . . the time is here now when the African writer must have the courage to determine what alone can be salvaged from the current cycle of human stupidity.

> The myth of irrational nobility (negritude), of a racial essence that must come to the rescue of white depravity has run its course . . .

> *Physician heal thyself.*[28]

This harsh recognition and acceptance of a difficult and dangerous commitment was especially hard for those writers whose driving impulse had, so recently, been to repair the trauma of colonialism. Much

Commonwealth literature of the past twenty years, often by writers driven into exile and published only outside their own countries – ironically, in the old imperial metropolis – subverts the bland unity of political conferences and resolutions; it is where the essential 'common culture' is preserved. The ideals of democracy and fair trial, of an impartial civil service, the rights of minority groups, of women, toleration of the right to worship may be feeble growths at present, but writers can keep them alive, contributing in the long run to the making of the better new nations dreamed of at Independence. If democracy can return to Argentina, and writers be rehabilitated even in Soviet Russia, why not tomorrow in Malawi, Kenya or Ghana?

I have stressed that the language is not 'everything', and I do not think Walcott himself meant to exclude English Literature, despite its insular limitations, from the Commonwealth inheritance. Yet the post-colonial backlash is not exhausted. The strongest plea for the eradication of English from the curricula of schools and universities has been made recently by the Nigerian authors of *Towards the Decolonization of African Literature*. They argue that, while the language must be tolerated as a 'temporary necessity', 'instead of being made to imbibe the imperialist and anti-African prejudices of England's literature, English should be taught to Nigerians through the English language literatures of Africa, Afro-America, and the Afro-Caribbean'; English literature should be consigned temporarily to a Department of Colonial Languages, itself to be abolished once English has been displaced as the official language.[29] The authors write as ardent pan-Africanists angered by what they see as the prolongation, after Independence, of English cultural hegemony in some African writers' 'eurocentric modernism' and in a Western criticism they find patronising, yet in their anxiety to clear the way for a predominantly African culture untainted by the old imperial order they condemn the literature indiscriminately. A more disturbing symptom of their narrowness than their sweeping rejection of all things English is their exclusion of all non-African influences: would Nigerian pupils also be threatened by *Indo*-Caribbean or Indian literature in English? It would be a sad irony if, when Commonwealth literature is edging into the school curricula and University English Departments of a multi-racial Britain, in the former colonies English literature were eliminated as a form of cultural imperialism. Fortunately, this seems an unlikely extreme, though the temptation to retreat into a cultural *laager* is an easier option than one which confronts critical contradictions and diverging attitudes and values in a Commonwealth dialogue that might serve as an example to the wider world. It is to be hoped, rather, that English literature will hold its place beside other world literatures in the kind of programme drawn up by the Working Committee elected by the 1974 Conference on 'the teaching of African literature in Kenyan schools'.[30]

The Commonwealth fully shares the world's problems of ethnic and caste discrimination, conflicting beliefs, social and sexual inequality, but differs in its possession of a common language. This has facilitated not an as yet inconceivable common culture, but direct cultural interchange and possibilities of increasing mutual understanding. These *possibilities*, through language and cultural links, however flawed, give the Commonwealth a potent advantage over the Babel of the larger world in seeking to reconcile differences. Beyond may rise the 'new architecture' the Guyanese writer Wilson Harris envisions, which would indeed be nothing less than 'everything':

> The new architecture of the world must be a profound understanding and revelation of all factors that combine into the phenomenon of effort and achievement not for one race of men but for all mankind together. Not simply for a glorious name or tradition in the historical sense but for an identity that is purposive and vital in a universal and manifestly human sense.[31]

NOTES

1. London, 1986, p.171.
2. Ngugi, 'On Writing in Gikuyu', *Research in African Literatures*, 16:2 (Summer 1985). It should be noted that Gikuyu, while it is the language of the dominant tribal group in Kenya, is only one of several national languages, the main one being Swahili. Ngugi has urged, 'we should express ourselves fully in those national languages instead of expressing ourselves in a foreign language like English' ('An Interview with Ngugi', *The Weekly Review*, 9 Jan. 1978: quoted in A. Gérard, *African Language Literatures*, 1981, p.313).
3. Ngugi wa Thiong'o, *Decolonising the Mind*, London, 1986, p. xi.
4. *Twentieth Century Jamaica*, Kingston, Jamaica, 1913, p.57.
5. See Nancy Foner, *Jamaica Farewell: Jamaican Migrants in London*, London, 1979, p.41. 'We didn't feel strangers in England. We had been taught all about British history, the Queen and that "we belonged" '. But they did not: 'When I got there it was a shock. A shock to discover people knew nothing about us. I discovered we weren't a part of things. My loyalty at age 15 was to England. I felt that Jamaica was part of England. The shock was to find I was a stranger'.
6. *Decolonising the Mind*, p.102.
7. From *In a Green Night: Poems 1948-60*, London, 1962. Walcott was writing during the Mau Mau Emergency in Kenya.
8. *History of the Voice*, London 1974, p.8.
9. *ibid.*, p.13.
10. *ibid.*, p.12.
11. *Jamaica* London 1973, p.11.
12. *History of the Voice*, pp.8-9, and Achebe, *Morning Yet on Creation Day*, London, 1975, p.56.

13. *Decolonising the Mind*, p.12.
14. *The Middle Passage* (1962), Harmondsworth, 1969, p.78.
15. *The Pleasures of Exile*, London, 1961.
16. *From Columbus to Castro*, London, 1970, p. 502.
17. 'Roots', *Bim*, No. 37, July-Dec. 1963, p.17.
18. *Maps*, London, 1986, p.172.
19. D. Walcott, 'The Muse of History' in *Is Massa Day Dead?*, New York, 1974.
20. 'The African Writer and the English Language', *Morning Yet . . .*, p.56.
21. *ibid*, p.62.
22. Plainly racist writers, such as Rider Haggard, Nicholas Monsarrat, Elspeth Huxley are on the margins of literature as studied and discussed, but have doubtless influenced popular white attitudes.
23. See Achebe's 'An Image of Africa', *Research in African Literatures*, (9:1 1978), pp.1-15, and my 'Conrad and Caliban', *Encounter*, March 1986.
24. See D. Dabydeen, ed., *The Black Presence in English Literature*, Manchester, 1985.
25. For recent examples see my review article, 'Fictions of Freedom', *Encounter*, May 1987.
26. 'A Small Personal Voice' in T. Maschler, ed., *Declaration*, London, 1957, p.24.
27. *Apology for Heroism*, Bombay, 1946, p.93.
28. 'The Writer in an African State', *Transition* 31 (June/July 1967), p.13.
29. Chinweizu, Onwuchekwa Jemie & Ibechukwu Madubuike, *Towards the Decolonization of African Literature*, Vol. 1, Enugu, 1980, pp. 205-6.
30. *Decolonising the Mind*, pp. 96-101. The vexed issue of competing tribal languages in African countries is beyond this paper's scope, but where this competition exists the life of English is likely to be prolonged, at least for pragmatic reasons – decreasingly for creative expression, e.g. Malawi, where *three* national languages include English; in Tanzania, on the other hand, the predominance in East Africa of Swahili is at the expense of English.
31. *Tradition the Writer and Society*, London, 1967, p.9.

5: ALASTAIR NIVEN
The Commonwealth Poetry Prize

With its high-sounding name and prestigious backing, it is surprising that the Commonwealth Poetry Prize is not better known. It has been awarded every year since 1972, except once when the judges unanimously decided to withhold the Prize rather than to debase it by giving it to an undeserving entrant. In this time it has rarely been used to honour writers already well-known for their literary achievements. Indeed, until 1985 when the rules were changed, it was only possible for first-time authors to win – those who had not previously had a whole collection of poetry published. The change of rules has allowed veterans such as Lauris Edmond, Michael Longley and George Barker to be in contention for the award. There remains, however, every inducement for the poet who is little known outside his or her country to be seriously considered. The Commonwealth Poetry Prize has always allowed its judges to go on a voyage of discovery through both charted and uncharted waters. Of all the literary prizes with which I have had something to do, it offers the most adventurous possibilities.

The simple rules of the Prize until 1985 meant that a single overall winner was being sought. There was thus great excitement in the homeland of the winning poet when the result was announced, but inevitably little attention elsewhere. The Commonwealth spirit is not yet so generous that the people of Accra and Sydney are going to be wild with excitement at the success of a writer from Kingston or New Delhi. Under the new arrangements, however, poets are nominated on a regional basis for books they have had published in the previous year. There is thus a winner for Africa, the Americas (Canada and the Caribbean), Asia, Australasia/Pacific, and United Kingdom/Europe. From these five area winners is selected an overall winner as well as a winner for the best first book of poems. There is no reason why the overall winner of the Prize should not also be a newly published poet, but in practice it is more likely that it will now be a well-established writer. For this reason it is good that the capacity to recognise newly arrived writers has been retained in the special award for 'first-time published poets'.

Not only were the entry rules remodelled in 1985 but sponsorship of the Prize was greatly enlarged. Today it would be impossible to run an international literary award without considerable sponsorship, and in the case of the Commonwealth Poetry Prize it has undoubtedly allowed the judges and the winning poets to travel, greater publicity to be provided, and prize money appropriate to the status of the award. There is a danger, however, that each literary prize will try to outmatch the others in the scale of its largesse, so that the situation which now prevails in big sporting events will come to dominate. It would be sad if the pursuit of money, which so often seems to have made good sportsmanship seem outmoded, should also come to prevail in the search for excellent poetry. There are also more immediate practical dangers in developing a sponsorship policy. The choice of sponsor can in itself lead to problems. Until 1984 the sponsor of the Commonwealth Poetry Prize, albeit to the tune of only £500 – the administrative costs being borne by the Commonwealth Institute in London – was the Diamond Trading Company (Pty) Ltd. I am surprised that none of the entrants ever took a stand over the source of the award money they sought, since its South African links were overt. Perhaps they did not know, for it was never widely publicized – but sponsorship which provides the sponsor with minimal public recognition and the administrator with furtive embarrassment is not the best kind to seek.

There was no such awkwardness over the sponsorship of British Airways, who took on the Prize between 1985 and 1987. But the fact that this source of sponsorship lasted for such a short time points out the fickleness and arbitrariness of the sponsorship world. Government encouragement to seek commercial patronage is especially strong in Britain, and increasingly so in other Commonwealth countries. It can seldom, however, provide long-term financial protection and there is a real danger of the enterprise which is sponsored being left high and dry if, as happened in 1987 with the Commonwealth Poetry Prize, the sponsor does not renew the arrangement – and, indeed, does not even in the period of sponsorship give much imaginative commitment to it. British Airways, for example, resisted the idea that they should publish Commonwealth poems in their in-flight magazines, which would have been a simple way of promoting the Prize and of assisting new writing. Fortunately a new sponsor, Dillons Pentos, has taken on the Commonwealth Poetry Prize, and the Commonwealth Institute has re-stated its commitment, so for the moment the Prize is safe again. The involvement of one of the fastest expanding booksellers in Britain seems appropriate and I shall be surprised if the relationship is not healthy both for Dillons and the Prize.

The Commonwealth Poetry Prize has been given mainly to young writers, inevitably so in the years in which it was only open to first-time authors. Indeed, quite a large eyebrow was raised when Gabriel Okara won in 1979, because it was felt that he had been a seminal influence in the development of modern Nigerian writing for at least thirty years. It transpired, however, that he had been extraordinarily careless in assembling the best of his work and that *The Fisherman's Invocation* was indeed his first collection. There has been no consistency to the kind of publishing house which is likely to produce a winner. A few have been brought out by international publishers but one, Timoshenko Aslanides in 1978, was self-published, and two winners, Michael Jackson in 1976 and Brian Turner in 1979, were discovered by the same small press, John McIndoe of Dunedin, New Zealand. Two small European presses achieved prominence for themselves as well as their authors when in 1983 a co-operative called Caribbean Cultural International at Karnak House in London launched Grace Nichols, who is now regarded as one of the best poets in Britain, and in 1984 when Anna Rutherford's Dangeroo Press, based in Aarhus, Denmark, produced David Dabydeen's first collection. Not only were two Guyanese writers based in Britain recognised in consecutive years, giving rise to the Guyana born Commonwealth Secretary-General's observation at the Dabydeen presentation that his country was colonizing the colonizer, but the small press movement was honoured by the award. It is extremely difficult for small publishers to get known and it has been an unsung achievement of the Commonwealth Poetry Prize that it has brought so many to wider attention.

There have been few patterns established by the Commonwealth Poetry Prize, but each winner has made an exceptional contribution to his or her national literature. It may not be as well known a prize as the Nobel Prize for Literature – nor will it ever be, as the eligibility is limited to Commonwealth citizens and the prize money is much smaller – but it has encouraged some unknown talents and confirmed the stature of a few poets who previously only had a local reputation. That is no mean achievement in only sixteen years. Every winning entry has improved the sales of that particular text immeasurably and in most cases the book has sold out within a short time of the award being announced. The job of literary prizes is partly to stimulate public consciousness of minority-interest writers; the Commonwealth Poetry Prize has done this with some success, though its existence is still rather too patchily known.

The Commonwealth Institute has always played a crucial role in the administration of the Prize. This continues. Indeed, when after the withdrawal of British Airways from sponsorship the future of the Prize seemed highly uncertain, it was the assurance of Institute support by its Director, James Porter, which kept the concept alive until new arrangements could be negotiated. In the early days the Commonwealth Institute shared responsibility for the promotion of the Prize with the National Book League (now the Book Trust) and with the Poetry Society. Today it handles most of the administrative procedures itself. The task is on a wholly different scale from sixteen years ago. In 1972, the year of its inception, the Prize attracted only sixteen entries. Now there are over four hundred annual submissions. Most of these are read with great seriousness though every crop produces one or two risible efforts which help to make the long judging sessions merry.

Let me describe how the judging takes place. Between 1972 and 1984, the last year under which the old rules were valid, I was on the panel eleven times. Under the new method I have been a judge only once. I think it is right to vary the panels of judges as much as possible and this has proved easier to do with the regional system now in operation. Since 1985 each regional panel has sent its Chairman to London to be part of the grand jury's final deliberations about an overall winner. Previously there was not enough money to fly people in from other countries and so the panel comprised specialists in Commonwealth writing who were available in Britain. Inevitably the same names often recurred, though conscientious efforts were made to create teams which were mixed in national backgrounds and in kinds of literary experience. It has always been a policy to combine writers and critics in these panels, but in the years before 1985 most of the writers selected were *deraciné* by virtue of their living in London, and it is therefore a moot point as to how representative of their culture of origin they actually were.

The formal judging sessions at the Commonwealth Institute are preceded by lunch, and I do not recall on any of these occasions anything being said speculatively about the decision-making that lay ahead. But the moment the coffee was finished we began our debate. Some years it was basically over in minutes because the agreement of the judges was evident from the start. On at least one occasion the judges were sent away and reconvened a week later having re-read several contentious entries. However the discussion which precedes it always, in my experience, began in the same way – with each judge slapping his or her personal shortlist upon the table and then swivelling their eyes around the table to see if their choice had been anyone else's. There was no previous collusion among the judges, who made up their shortlists unguided, but it was in fact rare not to find the same three or four books appearing in every judge's selection. There would usually be a formal discussion of every entry, with occasional lingering over someone's favourite choice which inexplicably everyone else had ignored – or perhaps some commendation to an unpracticed but arresting new talent which clearly could not be in the running for the main Prize. Discussion would follow about the agreed few who were front runners for the Prize. On no occasion has there been acrimony over the choice of the winner, though it would not be true to say that the choices have always been unanimous. Indeed, there has always been a point in the deliberations when the judges have had to think afresh about their criteria for judgement. Are they looking for the most technically adventurous poet, or the most deeply felt, or, in words I remember Fleur Adcock using, 'the most sculpted'? Should the writer obviously reflect his or her own indigenous or national culture, be evidently a Commonwealth writer with cross-continental interests, or show some abstract capacity for mastering poetic diction which eludes a sense of place? Are the judges being Eurocentric, paternalistic, sentimentally pro-ethnic, purist or ignorant? Every panel of judges has in the end resisted the notion of being prescriptive and, as a consequence, almost every kind of poet has now won the award.

Sometimes the panel has been faced with a real divide, as I believe it was in 1979 when the Prize was eventually shared between Gabriel Okara from Nigeria and Brian Turner from New Zealand. This particular choice highlighted the difficulties which to some extent all literary juries must face – what to do when one part of the panel has no knowledge of or access to the cultural *milieu* of one of the leading contenders? There is nothing reprehensible about being in this position: no-one can be expected to have familiarity with all the cultures of the Commonwealth. Sometimes it is possible to find common ground in some kind of universality, but it is often a tenet of major Commonwealth writers that they reject such a notion and aim for highly concentrated particularity. Where in the end are the common links between a Nigerian poem derived from Ijaw orality and the meticulous linguistic exactitude of a New Zealand nature observer? This is a crucial question which the new rules, whereby several regions of the Commonwealth nominate a finalist, do little to resolve.

Under the new arrangements, the Commonwealth Poetry Prize is open to all poets who are currently citizens of the Commonwealth. Britain is no longer excluded. Formerly the view prevailed that if British poets were allowed to enter then the Prize would be swamped by quantity and overpowered by quality. At one time I probably shared this paternalistic opinion, but if so it was many years ago. Since the rules were altered,

British writers of the calibre of Geoffrey Hill, Iain Crichton Smith and George Barker have been entered for the award (though Hill, like Seamus Heaney, hastily withdrew himself when he found out what his publisher had been up to – only just in time, as it happened, for he had already been selected as a regional winner and had no wish to go forward to the final stage). There is so far no sign of Britain submerging the rest of the entrants. No one fears to put Commonwealth fiction beside British fiction when the Booker Prize is awarded, and often it has been the Keri Hulmes, V. S. Naipauls and Thomas Keneallys who bring that one home.

The Commonwealth Poetry Prize now permits entries in translation, the rubric stating that such works 'will be judged on the artistic merit of the translation'. I am doubtful if any such entrant will win the Prize, however. Who is to assess a Greek Cypriot poet in translation, or a Zulu praise poet, or a Singaporean writing in Mandarin Chinese? Specialists could be invited to do so, but a whole panel would not have the expertise to adjudicate the merits of these poets besides those who originate their work in English. It might be better for the organizers and sponsors of the Prize to consider introducing a special award, comparable to that for the best first-time published poet, which would go to the outstanding translation into English of work by a writer who uses another Commonwealth language. These poems in translation would not have to compete with poems created in English.

Problems of eligibility for the Prize are perennial. I remember, when the credentials of one poet were being challenged at a judging session, insisting that it was the organizers' job to vet the entrants and that if anyone survived to the point that they were in serious contention for the award then it was not our job as judges to rule them out on a technicality. But the issues are not really as cut and dried as that. The Commonwealth is a place of great mobility. Timothy Holmes, for example, who won the Africa area award in 1985, is a white South African by birth who has settled in Zambia. So naturalization is an acceptable criterion for entry. But what, in the days before British entrants were permitted, could one make of a Londoner who had worked for five years with his company in Hong Kong? He, surely, could not enter on the coat-tails of being a Hong Kong resident, could he? Another cut and dried case, perhaps. There could be less easy examples, however, including that of George McWhirter, whose restrained and sensitive *Catalan Poems* shared the Prize in 1972 with Chinua Achebe. McWhirter, who was teaching creative writing at the University of British Columbia at the time, was born in Belfast and only by immigration was he a Canadian poet. His predicament in fact helped to ensure that the rules of the Prize evolved pragmatically. McWhirter was regarded as sufficiently rooted in the Canada of his adoption to be a worthy Commonwealth participant. With British entry now permitted that situation will not rise again, but the case of the South African in Botswana, or the American in Canada, or the Pakistani whose poems were mainly published when his country was a part of the Commonwealth, still arises from time to time in order to test the diplomacy and commonsense of the organizers.

Since the first year of the Prize, African entries have been infrequent, which seems to betray evidence either that the advertising of the award is not reaching Africa or, more probably, that African writers are going through a period of conscious insularity in which the internationality of the Commonwealth seems an irrelevance. Indeed, one has to wonder sometimes if the designation 'Commonwealth' in the title of the Prize is no: a disincentive for entrance for quite a number of poets and publishers, who in various ways do not adhere to Commonwealth ideals or who, despite the existence of the Prize itself as tangible evidence against such a view, regard the cultural interchange of the Commonwealth as a fiction. Africa's writers are probably the least responsive in the Commonwealth to the notion of a shared cultural citizenship brought about by virtue of Commonwealth membership, and despite having produced three winners in the competition the number of entries submitted from Africa has been almost derisory.

The fact that the three African victors, Chinua Achebe, Gabriel Okara and Niyi Osundare, have all shared the Prize with writers from other areas of the world rather than winning it outright, highlights the difficulty of the judges in finding a common approach to unfamiliar cultures. African writers do not like to be evaluated only in Eurocentric terms and it may be partly for that reason that so few of them have entered for Commonwealth literary competitions. Osundare's win, with poetry combining on the one hand great respect for the forms and lore of the oral tradition and on the other hand the energetic radicalism of youth, may encourage the younger African poets to enter the competition. Certainly if it is to attract more African writers of substance the Prize will have to appeal to the growing number of indigenous publishing houses in Africa.

This article is concerned with the issues that have faced those responsible for the flowering of the Commonwealth Poetry Prize. Space does not allow a critical appraisal of the writers who have won the award or been commended by it. The list of winners which appears at the end, however, indicates that they have come from many parts of the world. This has occasionally given rise to the suspicion that a Nobel-like principle operates, whereby there is an almost ritualistic selection of candidates as much for their place of origin as for their intrinsic quality. Such fears are ungrounded. It has only been by good fortune that the range of winners has been truly Commonwealth-wide. If there had ever been a suggestion that the Commonwealth Poetry Prize should be awarded by rotation then it is unlikely that Australia would have had it three times between 1978 and 1982 or that Guyana would have taken it in consecutive years in 1983 and 1984. To date, of the major areas of the Commonwealth only the South Pacific, East Africa and the European territories have not won the overall Prize, though under the old rules poets such as Western Samoa's Albert Wendt, Uganda's Richard Ntiru (commended in 1972) and Kenya's Jared Angira were pressing hard, and under the new rules several British poets have made an incisive mark. The judges show no signs at all of pre-determining their results. Nevertheless, the fact that the Prize has been spread around the Commonwealth in the sixteen years of its existence has undoubtedly enhanced its credibility. There is also evidence that when a poet has won the Prize his country as a whole benefits in terms of heightened recognition for literature. There are increased sales of the writer's books and plenty of media and bookshop coverage locally. The problem is extending this media attention to other parts of the Commonwealth which have no connection with the winning writer.

The Commonwealth Poetry Prize has undoubtedly given a fillip to those who have won it and to Commonwealth poetry in general. I leave open the question of whether literary prizes in the end do much good. They are certainly fashionable at the moment. The Commonwealth Foundation in 1987 instituted, again with the Book Trust's assistance, a new Commonwealth Writers' Prize – confusingly described, for it covers fiction rather than writing in all genres. This is excellent news and one hopes to see the poetry and fiction awards develop in harmony, even eventually in partnership. For the writers who win such prizes, sales of their books are bound to go up, they will be in great demand for readings and they are assured of a place in anthologies and in at least the footnotes of Commonwealth literary histories. Though there is not as yet much evidence that the Commonwealth Poetry Prize arouses public interest in the way that the Booker Prize in England and Prix Goncourt in France do, there is evidence that notice is taken of who wins each year, not least by teachers who are looking for new writing to introduce into the classroom or tutorial. There are, of course, purists who resist the whole razzmatazz that goes with honouring writers – the press releases, the photo calls, the award ceremonies, flying the winners and leading contenders to London for an Oscar-type presentation. I think that when the subject is new there can be great value in such a competition. Prizes also help to guide potential readers to books they might otherwise not discover. They are entirely defensible. They do, however, pose enormous problems of appropriate standards for judgement. When Dabydeen writes of 'White hooman walk tru de field fo watch we canecutta' he has only a distant umbilical connection with the New Zealand writer Michael Jackson's 'In a room of black enamel, gold/filigree, two schemed to love . . .' or even with his fellow Caribbean poet Dennis Scott's 'The heart's metronome/insists on this arc of islands/as home'. It is the fascination of a major literary award that it juxtaposes such writings and out of the conjunction can come surprising points of comparison and reciprocation. The Commonwealth Poetry Prize seems to have soundly weathered its early years and should be with us for many years yet, growing in reputation and influence. It is one of the success stories of the Commonwealth.

PAST PRIZE WINNERS

1972   Chinua Achebe (Nigeria) & George McWhirter (Canada)
1973   Wayne Brown (Trinidad and Tobago)
1974   Dennis Scott (Jamaica)
1975   No award
1976   Michael Jackson (New Zealand)
1977   Arun Kolatkar (India)
1978   Timoshenko Aslanides (Australia)
1979   Gabriel Okara (Nigeria) & Brian Turner (New Zealand)
1980   Shirley Lim (Malaysia)
1981   Philip Salom (Australia)
1982   Philip Goldsworthy (Australia)
1983   Grace Nichols (Guyana)
1984   David Dabydeen (Guyana)
1985   Lauris Edmond (Australasia/Pacific and over-all winner)
       Timothy Holmes (Best First-Time Published Poet, from Zimbabwe)
       Kobena Eyi Acquah (Africa)
       Gary Geddes (Americas)
       Vikram Seth (Asia)
       Michael Longley (UK/Europe)
1986   Vikram Seth (Asia and joint over-all winner)
       Niki Osundare (Africa and joint over-all winner)
       Vicki Raymond (Best First-Time Published Poet, from Australia)

Lorna Goodison (Americas)
Andrew Taylor (Australasia/Pacific)
Iain Crichton Smith (UK/Europe)
1987   Philip Salom (Australasia/Pacific and over-all winner)
Dinah Hawken (Best First-Time Published Poet, from New
  Zealand)
Tanure Ojaide (Africa)
Edward Kamau Brathwaite (Americas)
Keki Daruwalla (Asia)
George Barker (UK/Europe)

6: JOHN M. MACKENZIE

Conservation in the Commonwealth: Origins and Controversies

Conservation has become one of the linguistic icons of the twentieth century. Like most icons it is shiny, untouchable, reverence-inducing, but still gathers dirt. Governments pay lip service, but sin as soon as they turn away. Individuals pollute and destroy while professing belief. This is not just because erring is human. Sometimes it is because, in both historic and contemporary contexts, conservation is more complex than the unalloyed good it is so often made out to be. Like so many areas of human activity it has invariably had class and racial overtones. One person's conservation can be another person's dispossession.

This is particularly true of the Commonwealth. World conservation has its roots in an imperial past. It was often nurtured in dubious circumstances and has left a legacy of bitterness in many places. Although UN and related agencies like the International Union for the Conservation of Nature (IUCN), UNESCO, the World Wildlife Fund (WWF), and World Heritage have given world conservation movements considerable international cachet the problems of balance between the needs of people and the human obligation to nature are as great as ever. This essay seeks to examine the historical background to conservation in a number of Commonwealth countries, especially with regard to the relationship between humans and animals. In doing so I hope to uncover some of these complexities as well as reveal some of the similarities and differences within the Commonwealth experience.[1]

This is a particularly interesting time to undertake such a study because formal conservation in the British Commonwealth is almost exactly one hundred years old. The first conservation legislation on a national scale in India was the Indian Forest Act of 1878, followed by the Elephant Preservation Act of 1879. The first resolutions regarding the preservation of game in the Transvaal (later part of the Commonwealth) were put to the Volksraad in 1884 and 1889, while the first effective piece of game legislation in the Cape was enacted in 1886 (though most of the game had been destroyed by then). In Canada land was first put aside for a national park in 1885 and the first park legislation dated from 1887. In New Zealand the first reservation of land for a national park was made in 1887 though the legislation required to constitute it properly was not passed until 1894. These four regions reveal very significant differences in the relationship between humans and animals. In Canada, blessed with a rich and diverse mammalian fauna, animals constituted a prime food source and a significant economic resource. This was also true of Africa, where the significance of game meat in the diets of agricultural and some pastoral peoples has never been sufficiently noticed. The game also acted as a vital underpinning for European advance, offering a considerable subsidy for European enterprise through ivory, horn, hides, and skins, as well as providing vast quantities of meat as an aid in conquest, settlement, and war. In India wild animals were a food source for some people, but the experience of the majority of the Indian peasantry in relation to animals was the constant need for protection, of stock and humans against carnivores, of crops against herbivores. In New Zealand a very restricted fauna led to the introduction of animals by Europeans, first as a food source, later for economic, sporting, or simply sentimental reasons, and to dramatic ecological imbalances that were entirely of human origin.

Conservation comes in a variety of forms. Its forebear was preservation, the concept of preserving animals in order to provide sport, generally for an élite. In this guise it is designed for recreational killing, an élite ritual designed to facilitate the social interaction of members of a superior or governing class, promote skills useful in war and produce through hunting display a visible expression of the social order within the natural environment. The first European efforts at conservation in the late nineteenth century, particularly in Africa and India, were of this sort, following a long tradition from ancient and medieval times, developed in England from the late seventeenth to the nineteenth centuries.

Conservation can also be designed for the recovery of a renewable resource so that it can be more effectively exploited. Here economics predominates over sport. Once again it is often an élite impulse, although in this instance there may well be a communal element and it is more likely that the benefits will be more widely spread within society.

Only in the twentieth century has conservation been developed allegedly for its own sake, the preservation of a wilderness in an attempt to recreate a natural environment as far as possible untouched by humans. In fact this type of conservation, as applied to animals at any rate, is comparatively rare. Excessive animal conservation can all too easily produce environmental degradation because of over-grazing or browsing. Most conservation requires careful management in order to preserve the flora and ensure that no one animal species predominates over the others. Such management is particularly necessary because modern conservation is usually about access. To justify public expenditure conservation has to be visible. Protected areas must be made available for human recreation. While people may no longer hunt or burn grass or fell trees they must be allowed to see, although the manner of their seeing can also be strictly controlled. In doing so conservation once more becomes economically beneficial, this time through an indirect form of exploitation, tourism. As with preservation, access has strong class and, on a world basis, racial overtones. Access is possible only to those with the leisure, the inclination, and above all the financial wherewithal, to achieve it. Thus modern conservation blends ecological concern with scientific study and economic benefit and public relations through tourism.

First it is necessary to explode the myth that conservation was one of the great goods handed down to the world by western civilisation. Conservation had been practised effectively by peoples throughout the world before being introduced in its western guise in the late nineteenth century. Hunting and gathering peoples everywhere have been at pains to see that the basis of their subsistence was not destroyed. One people in South India carefully preserved a large bird population in order to supply guano as fertilizer for their cultivation. Hunters in Northern Uganda used a system of 'blocks' and strict territorial segregation to ensure that over-hunting was prevented. The King of Nepal in the 1860s was an ardent conservationist preserving forests in the Terai for economic exploitation and attempting, not very successfully, to restrict British hunting activities. A few decades later the Maharajah of Kashmir, recognising the severe inroads on animal stocks made by the excessive popularity of tourist hunting in his territory, introduced conservation measures and divided up the hunting grounds into 'blocks'. Lobengula, King of the Ndebele in the area which is now South-western Zimbabwe introduced conservation measures during his reign and fined European hunters for infringing them. He effectively introduced the concept of 'royal game' for the species he regarded as most at risk.

Moreover, the relationship between animals and disease was noticed and effective measures were taken to control its spread among cattle and humans. In East Africa people had successfully created zones free of the tsetse fly through settlement, bush clearance, and control of vegetation through agriculture and grazing. This removed the bush cover necessary to the survival of the tsetse. The second necessity of the tsetse, the game on which the fly fed, was restricted to no-man's lands lying between the human political units. They were sometimes the product of war, sometimes of judicious settlement patterns. Either way they regulated the animal-human interaction. They were in effect 'reserves' open to hunting forays to provide game meat as an important protein additive to diet or as a hedge against famine when crops failed. Mzila, king of the Gaza state in southern Mozambique and south-eastern Zimbabwe, noticed the spread of the tsetse after his arrival in the region and adopted policies of bush-clearing and game-culling to control it. Again 'reserves' were left. All of these examples illustrate ecological management allied to a form of conservation.

It has been suggested that a new concern about animals and a developing interest in conservation arose from the study of natural history in Europe in the nineteenth century.[2] Natural history became a popular pastime; collections became *de rigueur* in museums everywhere; and great specialist collections were developed and housed on a national basis. The opening of the British Museum (Natural History) in London's South Kensington in 1881, significantly just as the New Imperialism was developing momentum, is an excellent example. Natural history also became an important school subject; schools collected specimens, and boys and girls were encouraged to collect as well. This collecting mania had its effect on stocks. Egg collecting or oology had drastic consequences for rare species. Competition among museums led to the search for rare specimens and animal skins for stuffing and mounting which placed some rarities, like the white rhino in southern Africa at greater risk. The study of natural history was capable of having a negative effect.

Nevertheless, by the 1890s there was a growing alarm about extinctions. The dodo, enshrined in a figure of speech, was in everyone's mind. The fate of the Great Auk in Scotland, extinct in the 1820s, brought the whole problem nearer home. The near extinction of the North American bison, so closely associated with the lore of western America, was seen by many as an alarming instance of the power of human greed. In southern Africa the bluebuck and the quagga had been rendered extinct, the first around 1798, the second in the 1870s. A number of extinctions had occurred in particular countries, although the species survived elsewhere.

The conservationists were, however, in no way even-handed in their approach to animals. Until at least the 1930s animals were, in effect, divided into three categories, the economically useful, those which demonstrated 'sporting' characteristics, and those which were defined as vermin. The approach to the latter was particularly interesting. Large

numbers of animals were unprotected either because they constituted a
threat to human life or because they acted as effective competitors to
human access to both the economic and the sporting species. The great
predators like lions in Africa, tigers in India, cougars in North America
came into this category, as did wild dogs, hyenas, jackals, and above all
crocodiles. While there might be grudging admiration for the big cats
and an attempt to assume their perceived qualities in lordship over the
environment, nothing but contempt was exhibited for the other creatures
classified as vermin. Every human hand was against them and many
authorities were complacent about their eventual extinction.

Thus humans, including the 'conservationists', made lordly judg-
ments based on 'moral' and sometimes aesthetic grounds. Animals were
classified into those which 'deserved' protection and those which did
not. Moreover, conservationists were happy to be involved in the
reorganization of nature around the world which seemed to be one of
the marks of imperial power, a capacity for environmental intervention
that seemed to define 'civilized advance'. There was great enthusiasm
for the matching of species to new habitats. This had been going on in
the plant kingdom since the sixteenth century and there had been several
celebrated examples in the animal world, the movement of the horse to
North America, the pig to New Zealand and elsewhere, the merino sheep
to Australasia and South Africa, and various breeds of beef cattle to the
Americas and southern Africa. Now it began to take place on a
widespread and complex scale with sport and sentiment looming as large
as economics in the transfers.

Many of these perceptions and activities of the age can be found at
work in the creation of national parks in Canada and New Zealand from
the 1880s. The founding of these first nature reserves also reflects the
conflicting human considerations and complexity of motive, only frac-
tionally idealistic, lying behind a movement so often depicted as an
unalloyed good. This is well illustrated by the origins of the Banff
national park (as it later became) in Alberta, Canada.

The arrival of the surveyors and builders of the Canadian Pacific
Railway in the early 1880s suddenly made the routes into the Rockie
Mountains from the Canadian prairies better known. Among the new
discoveries were hot springs at what became known as Sulphur Moun-
tain. In an age when bathing in, and the drinking of, warm mineral
waters were highly regarded for their medicinal properties, as well as
being seen as a highly fashionable form of recreation, it was swiftly
recognised that these hot springs offered significant commercial prospects. There was a scramble to establish the right of discovery and stake
a claim to these springs and it was as a result of this unseemly rush that

the Canadian federal government, aided and abetted by the CPR, was induced to declare a national park on the model of the American Yellowstone founded in 1872. The CPR was scarcely a disinterested party. The hot springs and the surrounding natural environment could bring vital tourist traffic to its rails helping to make the company pay in its difficult first years. Private control of the hot springs might well inhibit development. Under federal jurisdiction the CPR could itself play an important part in their advertisement and exploitation, particularly through the building of a great hotel. To a certain extent, then, the creation of a national park represented the triumph of large-scale over small-scale capitalist enterprise.

But the federal government rode roughshod not only over the claimants, but also over the rights of the Stoney Indians. They had been accustomed to use the warm springs and the springs had also played an important spiritual and political role as the location for meetings between them and their neighbours. In 1870 the Stoney Indians had been ravaged by smallpox. Half the population died and their area of settlement was reduced. Within ten years their important food source, the bison, had been all but destroyed. Soon they were restricted to reserves outside the boundaries of the ever-increasing national park and access to their old hunting grounds was denied to them.

To a certain extent the framers of the national park were influenced by the dramatic decline and near extinction of the bison (which they attempted to reintroduce from the United States) and the notion that other animals might be under threat. But the earliest wildlife surveys of the park made the clear tripartite distinction among the economically useful animals, the sporting, and the vermin. A report by a federal officer, W.F. Whitcher, showed no sympathy for the original hunters, describing them as 'stragglers and deserters from their own reserves' and argued in favour of sport hunting in the park to raise revenue. Animals and fish were to be introduced for this purpose while the vermin that would threaten them should be exterminated. Bears were acceptable because they were generally herbivorous, but wolves, coyotes, foxes, lynxes, skunks, and all the wild cats should be eliminated. Some exotic animals were indeed 'acclimatized' and fish stocks were massively increased. Hunting was permitted to a licence-paying élite and fishing was developed as a prime recreational function of the park. The national park, then, represented the imposition on the region of contemporary ideas about wildlife, the restriction of access to a tourist, white élite, the exclusion of Indians from former hunting grounds, and the confirmation of the powerful partnership between the federal government and the CPR. As the celebrated manager of the CPR, William Cornelius van

Horne, himself said, the hot springs were worth a million dollars. The park's origins have continued to be dressed in idealistic garb, particularly in Canadian official publications,[3] but however beneficial it may since have proved to be to the interests of conservation and the recreational needs of the Canadian people, its existence represents the power of certain nineteenth-century interests and beliefs and is essentially symbolic of the dispossession of indigenous peoples.

In New Zealand the first national park was also rooted in dispossession, but in a rather different way. Maoris under Chief Te Heuheu IV Tukino found themselves caught in a pincer between a rival Maori group and European graziers. The Maori chief Te Kooti had been defeated in the Maori war of 1869 and had moved into Te Heuheu's area. Te Heuheu asked for arms to defend himself against Te Kooti, but his plea was not granted. Te Heuheu also viewed with mounting alarm the encroachment of European graziers upon the three mountains, Ruapehu, Tongariro, and Ngauruhuo which had a special sacred significance in his territory. He feared a time when almost all their slopes would be alienated and Maori access would be denied. Accordingly in 1886 Te Heuheu, aided by a local missionary who was his son-in-law, issued pleas to the Government that the three mountains should be taken into national ownership so that their spiritual significance could be preserved. The offer of the mountains was accepted in 1887, although it was not until 1894 that the lands were fully protected in national park legislation during the period when John McKenzie, the Scot dedicated to thwarting the accumulation of large private land-holdings, was Minister for Lands. More national reserves were founded in New Zealand in subsequent decades though it was not until the 1950s that the national parks were given full statutory authority and organised properly.

The parks and national reserves were not, however, designed to protect indigenous flora and fauna in the first half-century of their existence. The faunal poverty of New Zealand led to the large-scale pursuit of 'acclimatization' policies, the introduction of exotica for economic, sporting, and sentimental reasons. Captain Cook had liberated goats and pigs to provide a food source. Many others were later introduced to increase the wild food supply. In the middle of the nineteenth century opossums and wallabies were liberated in the hope of developing the skin trade. Several species of deer, including the red and fallow from Britain, the sika from Japan, the sambar from India, the rusa from Java, and the wapiti and moose from North America, were introduced and many of them flourished particularly in the mountainous regions of the South Island. All together, 130 species of birds, forty of fish and more than fifty of mammals were introduced, as well as a vast amount of exotic flora.

The reserves and parks became overrun with these animals. The 'conservation' areas had in fact become settings for attempts to replicate the Scottish Highlands, the North American Rockies, the Alps, and the Himalayas. In some places Maori land rights were infringed, as at Tongariro. When Maoris seized the opportunities presented by pigs and rabbits they were dubbed 'poachers' particularly if they attempted to pursue these animals in national parks and nature reserves. In recent decades there have been attempts to redress the balance against exotica. Previously valued and protected imported species have been declared vermin and efforts have been made to eliminate them in some areas, particularly where they have had a dramatic effect on indigenous plants and woodland. Thus New Zealand national parks have part of their origins in Maori dispossession and the desperate efforts of the Maoris to protect sacred places from encroachment. They also have their origins in distinctively nineteenth-century views of animals and the efforts of settlers to recreate the conditions of Home and other parts of the Empire in their economic and sporting approaches to wildlife.

In Africa, the proponents of preservation and conservation were a combination of colonial governors and metropolitan aristocrats, all of them hunters. This group was allied to a scientific natural history establishment in the museums and universities many of whom were themselves hunters. Few of these figures restrained their own hunting activities, though they justified them in terms of scientific enquiry and sport. They attempted to stick to a code whereby only mature males were fair game, hunting should be highly selective (having regard to the quality of the trophy or the need for self-defence) and the mortal shot should be inflicted as soon as possible. Those who hunted for economic or, above all, subsistence reasons were deemed not to adhere to this code and their hunting was consequently legally restricted. Moreover, it was thought that agriculturalists should not hunt, that hunting among such people was regressive according to social Darwinian canons.

The objectives of these hunter-conservationists fitted well with the demarcation of land use which constituted one of the prime thrusts of imperial environmental policies. Human settlement and animal habitat should be firmly separated since it was held that the existence of the latter was inimical to the development of the former. This separation was not to take place on a local scale as in pre-colonial times, but by the reservation of large tracts of land for specific use. In southern, Central, and some parts of East Africa the demarcation of human settlement was further complicated by the delineation of 'white' and 'black' lands, in which the black lands often formed a buffer between the white and the game reserves. The latter were further sub-divided into those that were subject to complete conservation and those in which controlled hunting under licence (and therefore largely restricted to whites) could take place.

These policies were partly conditioned by doom-laden pronouncements in the 1890s about the rapid extermination of species. It was thought that the insatiable demand for ivory in both the Western and Oriental worlds was bringing about the total destruction of African elephant stocks. The notorious properties of rhino horn, particularly valued in the East though readily supplied by the West, were producing a similar fate for that animal. Hippos, valued for meat and leather, were at risk as were a host of animals exploited for skins, furs, and feathers to meet the fashion demands of an increasingly opulent western society. In all this southern Africa was frequently held up as an alarming example. Until this expansion of Europeans and the recognition of western demands by African hunters the region had been immensely rich in animal stocks. But as human depredations increased, animals that had been common as far south as the Cape Colony until the nineteenth century had retreated into the far interior. By the 1890s scarcely any elephants, very few giraffe, rhino, or hippo survived south of the Limpopo except in the desert regions to the west. The ostrich, formerly common just inland from the Cape itself and throughout the sub-Continent, scarcely survived in the wild, although the immense demand for its feathers ensured its extensive domestication by the 1870s. As hunters penetrated Central and East Africa in the late nineteenth century and supplies of ivory, hides, skins, and other animal products appeared to be stepped up, it was thought that the same drastic retreat to eventual extinction would take place. In the course of the 1890s rinderpest, introduced to the Nile regions through infected cattle from India, spread throughout East, Central, and South Africa to the Cape. Great herds of buffalo and the larger antelope like kudu and eland were wiped out, while many other species were seriously depleted by its ravages.

These events led to the conviction that territorial extinctions at the very least were imminent. The Germans and the British instituted an international conference on the fauna of Africa in 1900. The Convention which emerged from it urged the further exchange of information, the widespread introduction of game laws by all the colonial empires, and the creation of game reserves. The game laws were designed to exclude African hunters, now dubbed 'poachers', from access to game, much of the blame for its destruction being pinned on them. Game could now he hunted only under licence or by those officially exempt, particularly in time of war. Licensing ensured that access to the Hunt was largely restricted to the élite, although animals could still be used as an important resource system in time of crisis. The Reserves were often created in areas where human population had declined as a result of smallpox, rinderpest, or war, or where populations had been moved as part of a wrong-headed attempt to control sleeping sickness by separating human settlement from tsetse-infested areas. Another international agreement of 1933 promoted the further development of game laws, the growth of the reserves, and the beginnings of their transformation into national parks.

The result of all this activity was to create vast game reserves in almost all the British African territories. By the Second World War the reserves in Northern Rhodesia (Zambia), for example, covered 18,435 square miles or 6.5% of the territory, while those in Southern Rhodesia (Zimbabwe) covered 12% of the surface area of the colony. In Kenya there were 30,000 square miles of reserves and in neighbouring Tanganyika (Tanzania) a particularly large proportion of the surface area of the territory was devoted to wildlife. Yet the whole policy had been based on a misconception. The alarm expressed in 1900 had been to a large extent unfounded. The problem in southern Africa was real enough, but in Central and East Africa knowledge of the real extent of game stocks was very limited. Moreover, the extraordinary recuperative power of animal populations was little understood. By the 1930s the problem was not one of extinction but of over-supply. The problems of this over-abundance of animals had already been noted by missionaries, in Nyasaland (Malawi) for example, by the First World War. African crops were under threat. The extension of the land available as game habitat facilitated the advance of the tsetse fly and placed cattle at risk from the cattle disease nagana and humans from sleeping sickness. Several of the first game departments in Africa were designed not to conserve game but to control it. Large culls had to be instituted to protect crops and human life. In the 1930s over 1500 elephants per annum were shot in Uganda, more than 2,500 in Tanganyika, and in excess of 5,000 in Northern Rhodesia. By the 1950s excess game populations were producing severe environmental degradation in, for example, Uganda, while famine and widespread death from starvation was the lot of elephants in Kenya.

With the institution of national parks, in South Africa from the 1920s, in East and Central Africa from the late 1940s, the vast lands set aside for animals were frozen in perpetuity. Reserves had been an administrative expedient, which could be created or abandoned according to gubernatorial decree. National parks had a much higher status, having statutory authority, and were much more difficult to overturn. By and large they survived into the post-colonial period hallowed by a combination of international tourism based on the immense fascination of more affluent peoples for African wildlife and the belief of the new nationalist governments that the world wildlife movement had to be acknowledged and supported by all enlightened regimes in the modern world. As a result tracts of territory much larger than were really required to protect the interests of wildlife were kept free of human settlement and in many places African peasants, accustomed in the past to supplementing their diet from game meat, continued to be denied this important source of protein. In the course of the century the transformation of preservation into conservation had been matched by a shift in its support from an aristocratic imperial élite to a bourgeois nationalist, and often left-wing, ruling group. Few imperial policies have so successfully made that transition.

There are a number of reasons for the capacity of the conservation ideology to appeal to a broad spectrum of political opinion. In the years after the Second World War the creation of international wildlife organisations and of national parks throughout Africa and Asia seemed to be an important part of the brighter post-war prospect. The British Left had adopted conservation as part of its internationalist and environmental concerns. Ramsay MacDonald joined the Society for the Preservation of the Fauna of the Empire, formerly the preserve of an aristocratic and largely Tory élite. The Attlee Government developed conservation policies in Britain, passing the national park act in 1949. A new breed of radical governor, like Sir Andrew Cohen of Uganda, applied a fervent belief in conservation to their policies at the same time as they grappled with nationalist developments. Many nationalist leaders picked up the ideology from their mentors on the Left, for it was an internationalist cause on which people from several continents could agree. Julius Nyerere, for example, pledged his support for wildlife conservation in the Arusha manifesto of 1961.

Moreover, when independence came in the 1960s tourism seemed to be a very important part of the economies of the new countries. In East Africa, for example, tourism contributed 8 million to the Kenyan economy at independence, while in the late 1960s the value of tourism to the three territories Kenya, Uganda and Tanzania was at least £20 million. In addition to this, some governments found the separation of zones of human settlement and animal habitat very convenient for administrative, economic and ideological reasons. In Tanzania the policy of village collectivization led to the continuation of the notion of concentration of settlement pursued by the colonial authorities and many people were cleared out of game reserves. After independence the reserves often continued to grow. Tanzania's Selous reserve, which had covered 2,600 square miles when the British established it in 1921, expanded during both the colonial and post-independence periods and by 1975 it extended over no fewer than 21,230 square miles of territory. Throughout this vast area all human settlement had been eliminated and rights of occupancy removed. It was but one of several reserves and national parks covering 70,000 square miles or 20% of the land area of the country.

The Indian experience of conservation provides an interesting contrast. There conservation made a late start and was promoted mainly by the Government of India after independence. Conservation areas, partly as a result of population pressures, partly because of sensibly worked out policies, took up only a fraction of the surface area of the country.

Both the Mughals and the British indulged in spectacular large-scale hunts designed both for display and as a ritualized offering of protection to peasant cultivators. For the British various forms of hunting and shooting became the favourite sports of the imperial period. Each viceroy and royal visitor was expected to shoot tigers, destroy vast numbers of wildfowl and participate in pig-sticking. The vast literature devoted to Indian 'sport' reveals the extent to which it became an obsession for both the military and civilian establishments of British India. It was both a recreation and a symbolic expression of power, a means by which the élite could interact and come into contact with a large number of Indian auxiliaries in an appropriately hierarchical setting. Forest officers in the vast forest tracts (covering one quarter of the land area of British India) were expected to hunt to provide knowledge of an intelligence about widespread areas which were otherwise thinly administered. Hunting on the frontiers of India also contributed to this gathering of intelligence.

In the early years of their rule the British indulgently observed Indian hunting, but by the end of the nineteenth century they had appropriated the words shikar (hunting) and shikari (hunter) for themselves. They encouraged the hunting activities of the Indian princes as an important medium of the feudal relationship between them, but they dubbed all other forms of Indian hunting 'poaching' and, as in Africa, set about stamping them out. As they became aware of the decline of fauna they often pinned the blame on Indian 'poachers'.

By the twentieth century a number of Indian species were at risk. It had been necessary to protect the elephant since the 1870s. The Indian lion had been reduced to only 100 animals in a small area of western India. The Indian bison or gaur and the rhinoceros had been reduced to small numbers in remote habitats. But the tiger was still being treated as vermin and was being disposed of in such large numbers that by the 1930s its population was in steep decline and within twenty years of independence it was in danger of extinction. Although there had been some game legislation in the British period it was largely regarded as a dead letter as a result of inadequate policing.

Increasing alarm was expressed in the first half of the twentieth century. Forest areas were divided into shooting blocks to encourage preservation. The Society for the Preservation of the Fauna of the Empire became concerned about the Indian fauna from the late 1920s. The celebrated tiger hunter Jim Corbett had undergone his conversion to conservation by the 1930s and was issuing propaganda for it. In 1935 the Viceroy, influenced by the international conference on the fauna of Africa, held a wildlife conference in New Delhi which for the first time began to consider the creation of reserves in India. But these plans were overwhelmed by the events of the late 1930s and 1940s. The last fifteen years of British rule in India were fraught with civil disturbance, war, and communal strife. Wildlife preservation seemed a low priority.

It was left to the Government of an independent India to begin the establishment of nature reserves and national parks. The accession of the Indian states and the continuing explosion of the human population had led to the destruction of many private forests and game preserves, the shooting out of animals, and the decline in the numbers of certain species, particularly those with skins that commanded high prices on the world market. By the 1950s wildlife management had become part of Indian five-year planning. The India Board for Wild Life was set up and it proposed the establishment of eighteen national parks. The Wild Life Preservation Society of India became active in world conservation and issued the magazine *Cheetah*. Wildlife associations and boards appeared throughout India and several of the princely game preserves became sanctuaries.

In 1969 the IUCN meeting in Delhi declared the tiger to be an endangered species and the WWF raised almost two million dollars for 'Operation Tiger'. A census of 1972 concluded that there were only 1,827 tigers left in India and a total ban was placed on hunting and shooting the animal in the Wild Life (Protection) Act of 1972. Tiger reserves were established and by 1979, when a major International Symposium on the tiger was held in New Delhi, populations were recovering rapidly. Ironically the vanquishing of the tiger, which had been seen as an imperial obligation and vital social rite of the British in India, had been transformed into the rescue of the tiger as a symbol of the independence and environmental awareness of modern India. Yet the total area of all the sanctuaries and national parks in India came to a little more than 2,600 square miles of territory, just over one-tenth of the final size of the single Selous game reserve in Tanzania.

The Indian national parks, small as they are, have become an important part of Indian tourist promotion. Conservation plays an even larger part of the tourist effort of Malaysia. There British plans for conservation in the 1930s were perforce suspended during the Japanese occupation and it was only after the war that reserves and national parks could be created, albeit in the face of suspicion and opposition from both peasants and plantation owners. The George V national park (later Taman Negara) and the Templer NP were successfully established and were later joined by four others. Publicity about them has become an important thrust of the Malaysian tourist drive. It is an interesting fact, and symptomatic of the adoption of the conservation idea by nationalist governments, that it is one of the few areas in which imperial figures have continued to be commemorated after independence, as in the Corbett NP in India or the Templer NP in Malaysia.

This historical survey of conservation reveals a number of instructive aspects of the transition from colonial rule to the independent Commonwealth. The conservation ideal was one of the few areas of imperial ideology that could be adopted enthusiastically by independent governments and became a source of international consultation and understanding through the Commonwealth from the ex-Dominions to Africa and Asia. Yet everywhere conservation emerged out of complex and conflicting interests. It has often involved human dispossession and a deference to expert opinion which in retrospect has sometimes proved to have been disastrously wrong. Policies like sleeping sickness controls in Africa have produced effects opposite to those intended. But the high reputation conservation has always enjoyed has tended to obscure these facts. It is interesting that more restrained measures have been adopted in those areas, particularly in India, where conservation came late. Conservationists do well to remember that conservation often confers benefits on some groups, élite hunters and international tourists, while destroying the dietary or territorial needs of other less favoured peoples, often the original owners of the land.

NOTES

1. Parts of this paper are based on my forthcoming work *The Empire of Nature, Hunting, Conservation and British Imperialism* to be published by Manchester University Press. I am indebted to the librarians of the University of Lancaster, the Royal Commonwealth Society, and of the High Commissions of Canada, India, and New Zealand for help with much of the research on which it is based.

2. David Elliston Allen, *The Naturalist in Britain: a Social History*, London 1976 and Keith Thomas, *Man and the Natural World*, London, 1983.
3. See for example W.F. Lothian, *A History of Canada's National Parks*, four volumes, published by Parks Canada, 1977-81.

Further Reading

Crosby, Alfred W., *Ecological Imperialism: The Biological Expansion of Europe, 900-1900*, Cambridge, 1986
Hamilton, J. Stevenson, *South Africa Eden*, London, 1937
Kinloch, Bruce *The Shamba Raiders*, London, 1972
Luard, N. *The Wildlife Parks of Africa*, London, 1985
Osten, Richard van, *World National Parks, Progress and Opportunities*, Brussels, 1972
Stracey, P.D., *Wildlife Management in India*, New Delhi, 1966
International Symposium on Tiger, New Delhi, 1979

Size and Statehood: The Geography of Politics

What should a state be? To the public mind, a state connotes a realm substantial in area and population, durable over time, and responding to corporate concerns consensually articulated by its inhabitants. If few states live up to these criteria, it is generally felt that they *ought* to. Even large states often fall far short of 'statehood' so conceived: dissent between governed and governing leads to upheaval or tyranny; invasion or expansion conjoins peoples of incompatible cultures or conflicting aims; massive social flux submerges the continuity of national identity. States that lack or contravene these criteria seem defective or aberrant, misnomers for some other kind of entity – an empire, a colony, or a dependency deficient in qualities of nationhood. In short, the common image of the state combines sovereignty with nationality: the paradigmatic state is a nation-state.

Small states fail the test of substantiality almost by definition. How far smallness depends on area or gross national product or population depends on variables that shift with context and over time. This essay deals mainly with entities below one million, but many, even up to five million, do not measure up to the received image of a substantial state.

This image of the state is quite recent. Up to the mid-nineteenth century, the normative state was a 'small' entity – small not only in our terms but to people then, by contrast with great imperial realms such as the Hapsburg or Holy Roman empires. The ancient Greek and the Renaissance city-state remained the European ideal: in 1850 Germany alone contained more than three hundred sovereign principalities. Approximating to Aristotle's ideal stage – one where 5040 inhabitants could see the whole at once – such tiny entities were the rule, larger nation-states like Britain and France the exception. India and Africa, too, were congeries of small states.

Not until the late nineteenth century, as Europe's older nation-states increased in size and power and Germany and Italy achieved unification, did the small state cease to be the norm. Now even their continued existence was resented as an obstacle to the larger nationhood felt to embody the soul of a people and to give them their full potential. Because small states contravened this geopolitical ideal, centrist theorists like Treitschke and Ratzel advocated their extermination as historical necessity. So swiftly did nation-states gobble up smaller entities that in 1904 Joseph Chamberlain reasonably concluded that 'The day of small nations has long passed away. The day of Empires has come'.[1]

A few small states survived these engorgements; a few more came into being in the wake of Versailles. Not until after the Second World War, however, did small states again emerge as major players on the world stage. By the end of the 1960s, decolonisation had created as many small sovereignties as larger entities. Imperial devolution still hives off new small states, but the end of that process is now in sight; the total number of autonomous (wholly or partially sovereign) small states has declined from a 1970 peak of 100 to about 85.

In short, within this generation the small state has made a comeback unimaginable at the turn of the century. These states play an international role of consequence their size belies. Indeed, they exemplify the anti-imperialist ethos of self-determination – the view that every people, however few or impotent, have the right to express their corporate identity through their own chosen institutions. As Bernard Levin put it, we 'mark with reverence the feeling of a people that they *are* a people, however absurd their claims on the definition may seem to others'.[2]

Yet the new prominence of small states and the principles that justify their being have made little dent in the public image of what a state ought to be. Save for the quixotic followers of Schumacher and Kohr, the state remains paradigmatically large. Even those alarmed by super power might perceive the normative state as large enough for substantial economic and political self-sufficiency that sustains a serious national purpose. Smaller states, especially micro-states, are apt to be perceived as political gestures, whether worthy or farcical, kept afloat by international charity or local chicanery.

The history just recounted shows that small states fit the criterion of durability no better than substantiality. Most are barely a human generation old, many younger still. Only the few residual European buffers and enclaves vaunt an origin preceding the nation-state epoch. Certain small states are venerable as social units, but their sovereign status is more recent. (One exception is Barbados, more self-governing in the seventeenth and eighteenth centuries than many para-sovereign entities today). The very newness of most present-day small states makes them seem evanescent and insubstantial. We assume that they are apt to submerge as speedily as they have emerged. Common culture and common purpose sanctioned the nineteenth-century nation-state. Notwithstanding disaffected ethnic and regional minorities, consensuality remains their essential justification. The *raison d'être* of the modern nation-state is that its allegiance, not coercion, persuade citizens to share its symbolic identity and to pay it taxes, obey its laws, serve in its armed forces, and become socialised in its schools. (I am conscious how ludicrous this generalization seems when applied, say, to South Africa, or Indonesia, or Chile: the pacification of dissidents in such states is no proof of popular acquiescence). In Gellner's terms, the nation-state embodies the transition from oligarchic despotism over a voiceless majority to a democratically realised consensus among a large homogeneous and literate people.[3]

How nearly small states approach this ideal is hard to estimate. Smallness, isolation, and their need, as dwarfs in a world of giants, to assert their identities, induce inhabitants to link their personal identities closely with the state's own. And small states are less likely than large ones to suffer ethnic or religious cleavage – although when such divisions surface, as in Cyprus or Sri Lanka, they may be more crippling.

On the other hand recent emergence from imperial rule means that most small states endure Third World deprivations. Highly visible extremes of wealth and poverty, privilege and squalor, power and impotence, make consensus and democracy in many small states more pious principles than practical realities.

These negative conclusions should be qualified in two respects, however. First, the very smallness of small states gives their inhabitants an influence *vis-à-vis* their leaders denied to most in larger entities. Rulers known personally even to the poorest are unlikely to seek, let alone to succeed, to ignore or exclude any group from consideration. Leaders themselves are apt to retain an ingrained sense of communality and equity, even egalitarianism. Second, the propensity of people in small states to emigrate while continuing to play a role in their home societies both amplifies and complicates local consensuality.

Small states thus strikingly diverge from those qualities usually associated with statehood. Moreover, no sharp boundaries distinguish small states from small entities that are not states. Processes comparable to those that engender new small states often result in their demise as autonomous units. By contrast, large states seldom hover between being and nothingness; whatever ails them their staying powers are considerable. Amin's excesses have ruined but not removed Uganda; ethnic rivalries and tribal hostilities led to prolonged civil war but left Nigeria intact; even the savaged states of Central America endure as national units.

No such assurance augurs the persistence of smaller states. They have less in common with larger autonomous units than with non-sovereign entities of similar size, such as French overseas *départements,* Portuguese Atlantic island dependencies, Pacific Trust territories. Some of these are in fact on the verge of statehood; a few have recently reverted from it. Like most small states, these self-governing dependencies are mainly Third World territories of European conquest, indigenous decimation, foreign settlement, and creolized culture. A proper purview of small-state characteristics must take into consideration these non-sovereign entities as well.

Beyond being unlike images of modern statehood, and being liable to evanesce, what qualities do small states have? Few scholars give more than unsupported listings of traits, and whatever is said of some small states seems to be disproved by others. Their very smallness makes them hard to comprehend collectively. Because small states are usually far apart, have quite different histories, and are institutionally and culturally diverse, comparable data for them is hard to find. But two geopolitical features of small states do stand out: insularity and remoteness from power centres.

Most small states and quasi-autonomous entities are islands, parts of islands, or groups of islands. Only 24 out of the 85 small territories in Sutton's and 20 of the 79 in Harden's listings are not islands.[4] Most of these are only superficially exceptions, fortifying rather than violating the near-universal insularity of small states. The circumstances of all but a tiny handful are genuinely insular.

To equate small-stateness with insularity is still wrong though, for while the majority of small states are islands, the majority even of inhabited islands are not small states and unlikely ever to become such. Yet these latter islands share important sociocultural characteristics with insular small states.

Insularity itself is hard to define. A host of significant traits differentiate island states: there are large and small, oceanic and offshore, archipelagic clusters and isolates; some are homogeneous, others divided by sovereignty, ethnicity, language or culture. Remoteness goes hand in hand with insularity. A high proportion of small states lie far from the global power centres of Western Europe and North America. The majority are in the Pacific, the Caribbean, and Africa; only the exceptional European small states are really close to power centres.

These exceptions highlight one small state feature strongly linked with their insularity and remoteness: most of them are emphatically of the

Third World. In Diggines' summary statement, they share problems of poverty, malnutrition, indebtedness, and political instability with other Third World states.[5] The paradigmatic small state of our time is thus an insular entity of quite recent sovereignty and of Third World socio-economic rank. Of the member states of the Commonwealth, 27 fit this definition.

Yet if most small states endure persistent Third World difficulties and deprivations, they are not quite characteristic of that realm. The world's poorest countries include few small states. Most of them enjoy levels of living substantially above those of larger Third World states. Although they account for half of the world's sovereign entities, small states included only 7 of the least developed countries in 1982, in a UN calculation based on gross domestic product, the manufacturing proportion thereof, and adult literacy. Small states account for half the global total but only one-fourth of the least prosperous moiety.

In view of their minuscule size, small states might be expected to register extremes of destitution regional disparities in larger countries average out. But the opposite proves true. The dire and pervasive poverty that affects sizable, often land-locked countries such as Afghanistan, Bangladesh, Ethiopia, Malawi, Nepal, Niger, the Sudan, and Uganda is absent in most small states.

One effect of smallness is to dissolve the academic boundaries between economic and political issues and the social and cultural factors of a state. Economic, political, religious, kinship and other systems in small states tend not merely to overlap but to coincide; people expect every social act to have economic and political consequences, and vice versa.

But these socio-cultural characteristics have generally received little attention as aggregates. Studies of such topics as tourism, monoculture, diseconomies of scale, governmental costs and benefits, and small-state international relations are legion. But the sociological and anthropological literature of smallness deals for the most part with relationships at a micro scale. Research has focussed on small communities within larger societies. On the social dimensions of small-state life nothing comprehensive has been written. Anthropological studies of particular islands abound, but few of these are readily generalizable.

The top-heavy political and economic emphasis shapes the debate between those who denigrate and those who extol small states. Critics attack small states overwhelmingly on economic and political grounds. Some early analysts found in them useful alternatives to absolutist, centralised nation-states. But political precariousness and economic inviability – the lack of clout that led Churchill to term pre-Bismarckian German states 'pumpernickel principalities' – made small states

anathema to nineteenth-century theorists. Economic and political disabilities dominate the disadvantages small states, notably insular ones,
are held to endure. Even protagonists like President Gayoom of the
Maldives, who told Commonwealth leaders in 1984 that it was 'not good
enough for the small states . . . to be just well defended bastions of
poverty', term economic development 'the front line of battle'.[6]

By contrast, those who count smallness a virtue often emphasise social
considerations. Hence Schumacher's assertion that 'people can be
themselves only in small comprehensible groups', Selwyn's claim that
people want national units small enough to identify with (as against mass
anonymity), McRobie's and Max-Neff's emphasis on the human scale,
self-reliance, non-violence, and harmony with nature.[7]

Three clusters of socio-cultural traits tend to feature small states:
conservatism and adherence to tradition; the careful management of
enforced intimacy; and a pervasive concern with autonomy. None is
exclusive to residents of small states, but they are most prominent there,
especially where smallness coincides with insularity.

Those who live in small states cling tenaciously to familiar patterns
of life. Their settled conservatism stems from a caution born of long
experience with resources whose exploitation is severely limited by scale,
by isolation, and by physical and economic hazards beyond their own
control. These constraints incline residents towards maintaining continuity, practicing conservation, and hedging bets by taking on multiple
occupations.

Just as smallness cramps resource exploitation, so it puts many goods
and services beyond local reach. Small states cannot afford amenities
elsewhere taken for granted. Paved roads, electric power, piped water,
telephones may require equipment, capital outlay, or consumption levels
that exceed local capacities. These diseconomies of scale are not static:
advances in global technology progressively worsen small states' plight.
It is not enough to keep population stable, for social viability demands
even larger consumer markets. In large states big schools replace smaller
ones, health facilities centralize to accommodate sophisticated medical
facilities, services concentrate in ever bigger centres. Smallness deprives
small states not only of new advances but of once customary services
technology has now made obsolete.

Small states are as fragile socially as ecologically and for similar
reasons. Smallness makes them excessively vulnerable to demographic
change. The population of large states can fluctuate substantially without
serious damage to resource management or institutional structures. But
a small initial base and a precarious population-resource balance mag-
nifies such impacts in small states. A sudden or sustained increase from

lowered mortality or an influx of outsiders may exhaust the state's limited resources. A sudden or sustained reduction owing to lower natality, epidemic disease, or increased emigration disrupts productivity, resource maintenance, and social structure. Where local enterprises and services are already marginal, even small imbalances can endanger the fabric: the departure of just a few workers, school-children, medical personnel may close a factory, a school, a cottage hospital, and threaten the entire social structure.

The island-state of Montserrat, which lost one-third of its inhabitants to Britain between 1957 and 1962, illustrates these effects. A loss evenly distributed would have been serious enough, but selective emigration made it far worse. Ninety-five per cent of the island's secondary school graduates left within a few years. The departure of trained personnel and potential leaders crippled government, business and social services. In just one year, the Post Office and Treasury lost 70 per cent of their employees. 'Temporary' promotions barely filled the places they vacated, and incompetents were coddled lest they too leave.[8]

Mass departure, especially of the able-bodied young, not only cripples agriculture and idles arable land, it leaves behind a less innovative and dependent residual population unable to cope even with normal environmental vicissitudes or to sustain traditional social networks.

Well aware of their economic and social fragility, small-state inhabitants realise that major change risks catastrophic loss. Hence they often view innovation with profound mistrust and take most decisions conservatively. Since potential 'improvement' may entail an unacceptable shift in resource exploitation or in the scale of enterprise, they usually opt to conserve what they have rather than venture new development. 'Progress' may upset the delicate equilibrium of services and goods that is the lynchpin of community interdependency; short-term gains may spell ruin in the longer run.

The virtues of stability induce small entities to bolster traditional ways even at pecuniary sacrifice. Thus Orcadians rejected uranium exploration lest success leave their traditional farming and fishing economy in a shambles. Ecological caution similarly pervades life for the 1500 inhabitants of Barbuda in the West Indies. On this dry, infertile island, Barbudans holding and working the land in common sustain themselves by combining extensive grazing and swidden agriculture with fishing, lobstering, and charcoal burning. Periodic attempts by outside authorities to develop the island more intensively have foundered owing to environmental constraints and local opposition; meanwhile Barbudans secure their continued livelihood and resource base through the diversity and conservation-oriented quality of their enterprises. Communal ownership and shifting cultivation condemned by 'experts' as backward and wasteful are, in fact, well adapted to the local environment, husbanding an ecosystem which permanent cultivation would severely impair.[9]

In short, small-state conservatism encourages resource diversification in place of monoculture, keeps open manifold options against the failure of some, inhibits specialization in favour of all-round competence, maintains economic and social resources in long-term balance, and celebrates the virtues of stability and tradition.

A second consequence of smallness in states is that their inhabitants must get along with one another. Most of them grow up within an interdependent network where each person figures many times over. Though specific contexts change over the life span, relationships seldom concentrate on a single act or specific function but tend instead to be functionally diffuse and to last for a long time.

Small-state social connections interlock in the fashion Demos describes for seventeenth-century New Englanders:

> Imagine the bricklayer who rebuilds your house is also the constable who brings you a summons to court, an occupant of the next bench in the meetinghouse, the owner of a share adjacent to one of yours in the 'upland' meadow, a fellow-member of the local . . . militia, an occasional companion at the local 'ordinary', a creditor (for services performed for you the previous summer but not yet paid for), a potential customer for wool from the sheep which you have begun to raise, the father of a child who is currently a bond-servant in your house, a colleague on a town committee to repair and improve the public roadways . . . And so on. Do the two of you enjoy your shared experiences? Not necessarily. Do you know each other well? Most assuredly.[10]

Life in most micro-states still fits this description, and many small states also exhibit such multiple relationships. Because their geography imposes particularistic social patterns no longer common in the wider world, visitors to small states often gain an impression of stepping back in time.

The smallness of the social field, together with ingrained awareness of ecological and social fragility, fosters what I term managed intimacy. Small-state inhabitants learn to get along, like it or not, with folk they will know in myriad contexts over their whole lives. To enable the social mechanism to function without undue stress, they minimize or mitigate overt conflict. They become expert at muting hostility, deferring their own views, containing disagreement, avoiding dispute, in the interest of stability and compromise. In a large state it is easy to take issue with an antagonist you need seldom if ever come across again; to differ with someone in a small state where the two of you share a long mutual history and will go on being involved in countless says, is quite another matter. Not simply the small size of the state but the complexity and durability of most relationships fosters sophisticated modes of accommodation.

I am not suggesting that small states are all sweet harmony. To the contrary, bitter and prolonged factionism can have devastating effects. But partly because factional differences are seen to have such potential for damage, small state inhabitants often take pains to conceal or mute the hostilities they may feel. In discussion they seldom express opinions dogmatically and are reluctant to voice divergent views. Assertiveness is proscribed: public meetings may open with periods of prolonged silence because no-one wants to be the first to speak.

Such traits underlie the traditionalism outsiders often extol. But these traits are quite alien to outsiders' own ingrained modes of behaviour. For instance, British immigrants who aimed not to transform but to copy real ways in one of the outer Orkney islands nonetheless found themselves bitterly polarized against local inhabitants. Schooled in global norms of originality and efficiency, these assertive and forceful newcomers took over many community leadership roles, violating ingrained local norms of continuity, sameness, and avoidance of overt conflict. The Orcadian traditions that the newcomers had idealized were simply the surface features of embedded social traits that proved deeply antipathetic to their own ingrained individualism.

The would-be new Orcadians failed to realise how superficial was their conversion to traditional folkways whose personality components were invisible to them, and how deeply ingrained in themselves were the drive, individualism, and reformism of modern urban culture. Moreover, they wrongly assumed that to become full-fledged participants, it is enough to esteem a community's values: in most small states linkages are inherited, not chosen, on the basis of manifold ties of kinship and memory.

Bonds of family underpin small-state intimacies. Families generate most other linkages; kinship loyalties suffuse small-state economic, social, and political enterprise. Elites in positions of consequence and authority are bound to be interrelated. In large states the nepotic use of power or authority seems morally wrong. But where everyone is related personal involvement in public affairs is inevitable, nepotism unavoidable. Small-state citizens accept kinship relations as the warp and woof of public affairs and family favouritism as a fact of life. Theirs is a realistic perspective on how human beings normally conduct affairs.

Small states tend to mute intergroup tensions, like personal hostilities, which might otherwise become serious impediments to harmony and dangerous harbingers of a divisive future. Two opposing ethnic groups of equivalent size or power especially aggravate such tensions, as Cyprus, Guyana, and Sri Lanka variously illustrate. Perhaps the most cogent case is Fiji, where indigenous Fijians still hold 85 per cent of the land and after six generations still consider Indians non-Fijians. Numerically almost equal, Fijians and Indians confront each other in an island state whose resources are strictly limited and zealously protected. The constraints of smallness exacerbate communal rivalries, for everyone knows there is only so much – land, jobs, money, power – to go around.

What is remarkable about Fiji is how, until 1987, both sides normally glossed over the tensions induced by demographic shifts. As an Indian Fijian recently claimed:

> We have never had an outbreak of the type of communal strife that rocks many other plural societies. We live in peace and harmony . . . and we expect to remain that way. While other multi-cultural nations must contend with . . . violence, tension, suspicion, and hatred, Fiji moves ahead in an orderly and harmonious fashion . . . Resentment is never strong enough to destroy the bonds of under-standing, affection and tolerance that unite us as a nation . . . We may complain about each other in private . . . but that does not stand in the way of friendship, tolerance and understanding . . . The good engulfs the bad.

And how does this happen? Well, 'Fiji society is conservative. We don't really like extremists. They make us suspicious and uncomfortable'.[12] In short, as his ethnic Fijian co-discussant remarked, 'in a small country there is no room to differ'. The ensuing coup, though virtually bloodless, showed the fragility of communal accord and the depth of ethnic Fijian fears of the hegemonic changes the Indian growth rate seemed to portend. Ethnic tensions can be contained by personal familiarity, by a recognised need for co-operation, and by mutual fears of conflagration and outside intervention. But meanwhile no-one must rock the boat.

The role of small-state emigrants is a third special consequence of smallness. Emigration is a ubiquitous aspect of modern life, but it has long featured in many small states, as in small islands generally. The strength and durability of emigrant ties distinguishes small states from other cradles of emigration. Rather than being lost to their homelands, those who leave extend their boundaries, helping to bolster small-state economies, strengthen their autonomy, and resist unwanted change. The rapid exodus of many able-bodied folk may strain a state's stability, but remittances cushion the departure; migration and return become an established routine, working abroad a normal part of the life cycle. Few small-state emigrants stay away for good; many remain citizens. The effective number of Anguillans or Barbudans or Caymanians is more than double the resident population at any given time. Thus many small states survive as social entities when decline in numbers of residents seems to doom them. Periodic return of the absent fosters continuity and community participation.

Emigrant communities are variously supportive. Networks of obligation with homelands persist for generations amongst Cook Islanders in New Zealand and Papuans in Australia. Diaspora Guamanians in California and West Indians in Toronto retain or replicate much of their homeland culture, replenishing rather than diminishing it.[13] Emigrants whose education and economic success foster self-awareness often assert their national identity more strongly in exile than at home.

Emigrants contribute more than remittances and rallying points; their investments, their metropolitan contacts and concepts and their cosmopolitan energy and dynamism also reshape the home society.

Frequent movement helps returning migrants to fit in again easily at home. When many of a small state's citizens have experienced life abroad, it is less apt to be polarized between stay-at-homes and those who have sought wider horizons. Emigrants may see the homeland less as a place in need of development than as a haven from the metropolitan hurly-burly. While success abroad gains personal achievement, return reinforces local conservative and conservationist tendencies. Like tourists, returning emigrants are sometimes lured back by displays of traditionalism that may belie residents' own preferences for modern convenience. But even newly invented relics and contrived solidarity with ancient ways may in time become respectable features of small-state 'traditional' life.

Yet the small-state propensity to hive off actively involved migrant communities casts the boundaries of the state itself in doubt. With a network of Barbadian social and economic enterprises extending from Bridgetown to Brooklyn and from London to Toronto, is it realistic to think of Barbados purely as a small Caribbean island state? Barbados is that, to be sure, but it is also those Barbadians spread throughout the Caribbean and beyond. And from Anguilla to Ascension, Guam to Guyana, Sao Tomé to Suriname, most small states exhibit comparable overseas networks.

People in small states zealously guard their statehood. Yet statehood costs them dear. Small-state governments are both meddlesome and burdensome. In general, government's share of total enterprise varies inversely with state size. Any state requires an irreducible minimum of infrastructure, and the smaller the state the larger its government looms in its economy and society. The need to mount services that no private entrepreneur would afford further aggrandizes the government's sphere. Maintaining autonomy, both substantive and symbolic, likewise demands a palpable government presence. Small-state governments are characteristically top-heavy.

The omnipresent government moreover feels omnipotent. Its aggrandized roles make it a party to every significant enterprise. As it controls access to most skills and funding, no-one can move far up any ladder of enterprise without bumping into government. A small-state government can thus veto any undertaking that clashes with its own overweening prerogatives. Every entrepreneur must play ball with its leaders. This closes off many potentially attractive avenues of innovation.

The weight of government in small states exacts other costs too. One stems from the political personalism noted above. But there are graver problems than favouritism. Inhabitants of small states have virtually no recourse to impartial authority. Neither the civil service nor the judiciary can escape influence, if not coercion, exerted by political leaders. These costs were spelled out in graphic detail by W. Arthur Lewis in explaining why West Indian micro-states would be disastrous alternatives to a federation.[14] His arguments remain germane, though it is unclear how large a state ought to be to avoid such disabilities.

Yet however costly or coercive their governments, most in small states prefer these disabilities to those they would probably suffer should they lose their sovereignty. Even clustered among supportive neighbours, small states sense the pervasive pressure of nearby larger states and great powers. These outsiders not only interfere in times of crisis; they impinge on day-to-day livelihood and well-being, circumscribing small-state autonomy in countless ways.

Small-state self-rule is thus not just empty chauvinism; it offers a cohesion needed to bolster autonomy against the incursions of larger states, the pressures of global development, and the perils of piracy. To this end, small states inculcate attachments to anything national, everything that distinguishes them from other states, their people from other people. As Doumenge notes for islanders, they 'are never happier than when asserting they are completely different from their neigh-bours'.[15] Hence their ritual emphasis on endemic institutions and their exaggerated claims to cultural unanimity. Linguistic nationalism in Iceland and Ireland, the Faroes and Luxembourg, serves alike to exclude non-nationals and to buttress the sense of belonging among nationals.

Little wonder that small states sometimes seem paranoid about external subversion. Keeping outsiders from owning local land and other resources is a *sine qua non* of continued local control, essential for statehood viability. Barbuda's desperate effort to keep in force old ordinance affirming communal ownership of all local land by Barbudans alone is a case in point.

Small states thus safeguard what autonomy they have and strive to enlarge it. The bloated infrastructures of Nauru and Barbados, Sark and Man, are the envy of devolutionists in Brittany and Cornwall. Self-government is expensive, and the smaller the government the higher the per capita cost. But a measure of sovereignty yields manifold benefits. A state that rules itself can prime its own pump. Even an inefficient or venal government creates employment, generates business, and disperses funds. It can promote fund-raising schemes – stamps, coins, casinos, tax havens – seldom available to dependencies. Sovereignty also yields access to international aid agencies. When Grenada opted for sovereign status in 1968, the island's then leader, Eric Gairy, was asked how Grenada would be able to afford it. 'Grenada will not support independence', he answered. 'Independence will support Grenada'.[16] (At least it enriched Gairy).

Autonomy also buffers states against imperial parsimony. Larger states are often mean and grudging in doling out aid to outlying appendages, especially when diseconomies of scale make services there more costly. By contrast, a self-governing state can decide its own priorities, allocating funds for some services outsiders might think unnecessary, while forgoing other expenditures.

Most important, autonomous citizens can freely express and enjoy their autonomy, however self-inflated this self-image may appear to others. Self-government enables entities to arouse public protest, campaign against great-power iniquities, mobilize against takeover or abandonment. No wonder that Anguilla's 5,000 and Barbuda's 1,500 inhabitants sought sovereign status; that Orkney and Shetland warned Scottish devolutionists the islands might go their own way, taking North Sea oil with them and that Nantucket and Martha's Vineyard threatened to secede from Massachusetts unless the Bay State agreed to a federal bill to protect their environments from development. Indeed, deploying para-sovereign status against entrepreneurial intrusion is an innovation coveted by regional separatists the world over.

These small-state socio-cultural features are, on balance, more advantageous than otherwise, worthy of note and perhaps emulation in a world increasingly run by super-powers and multi-national agencies, too large and remote for most citizens to feel that they belong, let alone play any significant political role.

Small states generally get a bad press. Along with their problematic viability, they are arraigned as foci of global instability, touchpoints or power vacuums liable to ignite global tensions. These charges seem to be groundless. Great-power animosities generally come to a boil over global issues or larger states – Afghanistan, Cuba, Nicaragua. Small states lack sufficient infrastructure or room for manoeuvre to make them truly useful international pawns. And they are seldom loci of global lawlessness.

Small states have positive as well as negative virtues. Their existence enhances human diversity. Their sovereignty fosters the continuance of cultures of myriad kinds. Their instinct of self-preservation, narrowly chauvinist though it may sometimes seem, nurtures attachments to particular and uniquely precious lands and landscapes.

These diverse small-scale loyalties may seem anachronistic in a world dominated politically by giant states, economically by multi-national corporations, and culturally by global media. But global and mega-national identities do not suffice humanity, as revitalized ethnic and regional minority movements amply attest. Not all such entities would benefit from independence or autonomy, though many crave it. But cultures coterminous with small states express and sustain that identity better than can remnant peoples rendered impotent within nation states.

Sovereign status may belie a small state's lack of economic, social, or administrative viability or fail to sustain its cultural traditions against global homogenizing pressures. Alternatively, such a state may opt for modernization at the cost of its unique identity. But autonomy lends it two virtues: first, the state can be critically helpful in sociocultural protection; second, whether the choice is to modernize or to cherish traditional ways, the decision is more apt to be, and seen to be, made by the citizenry itself, not by outsiders.

In small-state affairs the Commonwealth plays a major role. In the first place, the British empire came to engross a greater proportion of the world than any other European imperial enterprise. Decolonisation thus left the Commonwealth, the empire's successor, with a giant's share of the world's sovereign entities, especially of its small states.

Secondly, British imperial rule and its devolution favoured greater institutional and cultural diversity and a deeper rooted tradition of local autonomy than the former French, Dutch, or Belgian colonies manifest. In the latter, assimilation within mainstream European culture long remained the sole goal of worth for local élites, and French centralism still pervades formally sovereign francophone states.

The small states of the Commonwealth were forged in a different tradition. It was profoundly racist in assuming Britishness a goal unattainable save by ancestry; and it was romantically misguided in assuming that colonial subjects long denied self-rule could simply be handed back 'traditional' modes of life. But it was also a tradition that operated more by indirect rule, left a lighter imprint on other peoples, and recognised that non-European ways of life and thought had an inherent validity worth nurturing. Thus the small states of the Commonwealth, notwithstanding their evident frailties, draw strength from a legacy that honours diversity and self-determination. It is a legacy they might well pass on to the rest of the world.

No-one would wish to preserve a small state as a museum piece in the modern world against its inhabitants' own wishes. But by the same token, no-one ought to seek to deprive them of that status against their will.

NOTES

*Parts of this paper appear in my 'Social features' in Colin Clarke and Tony Payne, eds., *Politics, Security and Development in Small States,* London: Allen & Unwin, 1987, pp. 26-49

1. C. E. Diggines, 'The problems of small states', *Round Table,* 74 (1985) 191-205, reference on p.204.
2. Bernard Levin, 'A nation for all that, even if it is just a dot on the map', *The Times,* 23 February 1977, p.1.4
3. Ernest Gellner, *Nations and Nationalism,* Oxford, 1983.
4. Paul Sutton, 'Political aspects', in Clarke and Payne, *op. cit.* pp. 3-25. Shula Harden, *Small is Dangerous: Micro States in a Macro World,* London, 1985.
5. Diggines, *op. cit.*
6. Harden, *op. cit.,* p.8
7. E. F. Schumacher, *Small is Beautiful,* (London, 1974, p. 68; Percy Selwyn, 'Room for manoeuvre?' in his (ed.), *Development Policy in Small Countries,* London, 1975, pp. 8-24; C.A. McRobie, *Small is Possible,* London, 1981; M. Max-Neef, *From the Outside Looking In,* Uppsala, 1982.
8. David Lowenthal and Lambros Comitas, 'Emigration and depopulation: some neglected aspects of population geography', *Geographical Review,* 62, (1962), 195-210; David Lowenthal, *West Indian Societies,* London, 1972, pp. 219-22; Stuart B. Philpott, *West Indian Migration: The Montserrat Case,* London, 1973.
9. David Lowenthal and Colin Clarke, 'Common lands, common aims: the distinctive Barbudan community', in Malcolm Cross and Arnaud Marks, eds., *Peasants, Plantations and Rural Communities in the Caribbean,* Leiden, 1979, pp. 142-59.
10. John P. Demos, *Entertaining Satan: Witchcraft and the Culture of Early New England,* New York, 1982, pp. 311-12.
11. Diana E. Forsythe, 'Urban incomers and rural change: the impact of migrants from the city on life in an Orkney community', *Sociologia Ruralis,* 20 (1980), 287-307; *idem, Urban-Rural Migration, Change and Conflict in an Orkney Island Community* (North Sea Oil Panel Occasional Paper, no. 14) London, 1982.
12. Shiu Prasad, 'Ethnic relations in island development: the Fiji experience', paper for *Islands '86* conference, Victoria, B.C.
13. Murray Chapman, ed., *Mobility and Identity in the Island Pacific, Pacific Viewpoint,* 26:1 (1985) Wellington, N.Z.
14. W. Arthur Lewis, *The Agony of the Eight,* Bridgetown, Barbados, 1965.

15. Francois Doumenge, 'The viability of small intertropical islands', in E.C. Dommen and P.L. Hein, eds., *States, Micro-states and Islands,* London, 1985, pp. 70-118, reference on p. 102.

16. David Lowenthal, 'An island is a world: the problem of Caribbean insularity', in Elizabeth M. Thomas-Hope, ed., *Perspectives on Caribbean Regional Identity,* Liverpool University Centre of Latin American Studies, no.11, 1984, pp. 109-21, reference on p. 114.

Further Reading

Amstrup, Niela, 'The perennial problem of small states: a survey of research efforts', *Co-operation and Conflict,* 11 (1976), 163-82.

Benedict, Burton, ed., *Problems of Smaller Territories,* London, 1967.

Cohen, Anthony P., ed., *Belonging: Identity and Social Organisation in British Rural Cultures,* Manchester, 1982.

Dahl, R.A. and E.R. Tufte, *Size and Democracy,* Stanford, Calif., 1973.

Isaacs, Harold R., *Idols of the Tribe: Group Identity and Political Change,* New York, 1975.

Seton-Watson, Hugh, *Nations and States: An Enquiry into the Origins of Nations and the Politics of Nationalism,* Boulder, Colo., 1977.

Wright, Ronald, *On Fiji Islands,* New York, 1987.

8: KENNETH PARKER
A Common Wealth of Difference

My starting point is that of difference – inevitably and inescapably – because it is precisely the notion of difference that is highlighted when one compares the theme of Professor Ramphal's lecture with the title of the collection to which it has given rise. The argument in favour of concentrating upon the notion of 'difference' does not arise simply because the theme of the lecture is to assert the sense of a 'common purpose', whereas that of the collection's title raises that of a 'common culture' (no matter, for the moment, how that term is defined), but more fundamentally, because one needs to account, in the light of the confident tone of the lecture, for the existence and role of the question-mark in the title page. To do that, it might be useful to restate, briefly, some of the key propositions in the lecture, in order not only to note what it asserts, but also to draw attention to what it omits, in relation to 'common purpose', before proceeding to say something about 'common culture' and its associated questionmark.

Leaving aside the sense of worldweariness ('. . . a world that shows signs of losing its way in the twilight of this fading century'; 'For the world community, taken as a whole, it is close to the worst of times'; 'The agenda of anxiety'), the following would seem to be the key propositions: firstly, that '. . . it was Britain's genius for political innovation that helped to give the world the modern Commonwealth'; secondly, that a 'functional definition' of the Commonwealth is that it is a 'facility for harmonizing differences, even contrariness, within the framework of community', since, thirdly, the Commonwealth '. . . represents the supremacy of community over otherness'.

The proposition that the British have a particular 'genius' for innovation in statecraft is as regularly proclaimed as it is challenged. The proposition is proclaimed by those who incorporate that assertion in the more general theory of a beneficent 'Mother Country', slowly letting go of the burdens of rule, by which theory struggles for self-determination and independence are marginalized. Thus, the popular British image of the recolonizing process is that of Lord Soames handing over power in Zimbabwe, or of the Earl Mountbatten of Burma doing the same on the Indian subcontinent; scant credit is given for the contribution of the indigenous peoples towards their own liberation – much in the same way as the popular history of slave emancipation is constructed around Wilberforce, Clarkson, and others, with only slight (and sometimes slighting) references to the role of black revolt. That construction is challenged by those who see the Commonwealth as a rather sophisticated structure for the continuation of domination on the part of a 'perfidious Albion'. While neither of these views can be comprehensively sustained logically, they are, nevertheless powerful conductors of opposing ideologies, and, thus, especially in their crude and antithetical form, they contain not only elements of validity, but become slogans for actions. It is precisely for that reason that they require interrogation.

Professor Ramphal is quite correct to draw attention to the innovative nature of British statecraft; radical critics are equally justified in pointing out the reasons for, as well as the role of, that innovation in statecraft in the management of patterns of domination and control. The model of crude political domination, unmodified by any vestige of consent or cooperation, is now rather outmoded, but the case for 'genius', extrapolated from context, is equally unsatisfactory. A valid case can be made for a British contribution to the art of statecraft. It can even be reasonably precisely dated as having its origins in the search for a form of government based upon the notion of consent on the part of an organised political community. While we now recognise that notion of community to have been restricted by gender as well as class, we also recognise in the heritage of Civil War and Revolution, in the writings of Hobbes, Locke, Milton, the debates at Putney, etc. the seventeenth-century origins of some present-day dilemmas.[1] It is not at all a paradox that genius for seeking strategies to incorporate and neutralize dissent at home should be used, at the same time, to effect dispossession abroad – the plantation of Ireland; the colonization of the Caribbean; the management of the slave trade. It is this sense of common purpose that the 'Mother Country' has sought to maintain throughout: in a trajectory from colony via empire to self-government and independence, 'common purpose' has, in each successive stage, been modified, as well as modernized, not so much to keep the former dependencies dependent, as to ensure that the dominant ideas through which that purpose is expressed are those of the metropolis.[2]

This process is not simply a matter of the extent to which the 'Westminster model' continues to apply in Canberra, or Harare, or Gaborone, but the extent to which the 'common purpose' depends upon a notion of a common rationality. But this assumption of the existence of such a common rationality, while hinted at in the lecture, is never spelled out. If the structures through which the 'common purpose' are· orchestrated are based in the belief in a common rationality, rather than of (say) custom and practice, then whose rationality is it? Which are the dominant ideas? How did these triumph over other, competing ideas? We shall need to admit that in order for the 'genius' to acquire hegemonic status, competing ones had to be suppressed – not only forms of rule and obligation, but also the mentalities, specific to those regions and groups, out of which those emanated. It is this process, as well as its underpinning ideology, rather than the more debatable charge of racism, that explains the British prime minister's attempt to impose her views on the rest of the Commonwealth with regard to 'South Africa'[3]; and the resistance on the part of other member states to those might therefore be seen as stemming as much from a genuine abhorrence of the ways of the apartheid white minority state, from a rejection of the hegemonic assumptions implicit in the particular utterances and policies.

More fundamentally, the assertion of 'common purpose' obscures another critical difference: specific and particular patterns of historical experience are either set aside, or skewed, in the interests of some over-arching internationalism. My argument is perhaps best illustrated by the interpretation of Commonwealth responses to 'apartheid' and to 'South Africa'. I should declare an interest here, as a black, born in what was the Union of 'South Africa'. It is misleading and inaccurate to assert, as Professor Ramphal does, that the white 'South African' government of Dr Verwoerd left the Commonwealth in 1961 because apartheid was 'seen to challenge also the basic tenets of the Commonwealth'. The basic tenets of the Commonwealth, as they now stand, especially in relation to racism, were significantly different at that time; the 'basic tenets' then were those of the 'Old', dominantly white members – only a handful of the 'New' (euphemism for 'Black') Commonwealth were members then, and the shift towards taking racism seriously as a global issue came much later. While it is true that many English-speaking white 'South Africans' opposed the decision to leave the Commonwealth, we must remember that their opposition was not because of their abhorrence of apartheid – their opposition stemmed out of a sense of cultural superiority over the all other groups in the common society, based upon a belief in the cultural supremacy of 'Englishness'; so that it is important to emphasise that, for the Boers, leaving the Commonwealth was the last great symbolic act of freeing themselves of the folk memory of British imperialism. That racial memory encompassed not simply the military defeat of the Boer republics but also their deep-seated sense of cultural oppression – though it could be argued that they were more than adequately compensated by the nature of the political settlement of the 1910 Act, which gave them dominance in the common society over both Brit and Black. And while we recognise the validity of their case, politically as well as culturally, we should note the paradoxical reason for their desire for 'freedom' – in order to better oppress the blacks (who were not consulted on the issue of continuing membership of the Commonwealth).[4]

The question then arises: would it have made a difference if 'South Africa' had remained in the Commonwealth? Assuming that a minority white 'South Africa' remained a member, would successive governments in that country have heeded the 'basic tenets' as these were being modified, fine-tuned? And had they not done so, how might the Commonwealth have acted to seek to ensure compliance? Commonwealth practice in response to recent events cannot be said to inspire confidence, if one judges now not by the resolutions of the Nassau conference or of the Eminent Persons on a State which is not a Commonwealth Member, but by responses to events in member countries – the Seychelles; Fiji. What price 'common purpose', or the operation of 'genius' in statecraft?

Perhaps that is why the second key point in the lecture – that of the Commonwealth as 'a facility for harmonizing differences within the framework of community' is stated as a functional definition – as opposed, one presumes, to a 'philosophical or 'theoretical' one. Such a definition begs many questions, especially that of the definition of 'community'. If the notion of 'community' has certain associations with distinct features by which we may distinguish it from others, whilst yet sharing a common habitat, then one is bound to ask how the notion of harmonizing differences, even contrariness, might be justified in the case of Fiji. If, as the Professor argues, the Commonwealth has this capacity for bridge-building in an international context, what were the sappers up to in Suva? This is not to deny or minimize the importance of definition by function; there is clearly an immense value as well as utility in the existence of the Commonwealth Secretariat and of many other Commonwealth-related structures and organs, such as the Commonwealth Institute and the Association of Commonwealth Universities, but the question must be how these fulfill their functions, and the answer to that cannot be divorced from some sense of ideology – whose notion of 'community', or harmonizing whose difference?[5]

Let me illustrate with what may be considered a trivial example: that elegant building situated so fairly in close proximity to salubrious Holland Park, the Commonwealth Institute, has a permanent exhibition of aspects of every single member country, even of places like Jersey and the Isle of Man. It also has a most glaring absence – that of Great Britain itself. School parties who go there can study the dioramas of each of these 'other' places, roughly equivalent to the manner in which they would look at dioramas in The Natural History Museum. The 'Commonwealth' is somehow all its member states, except Great Britain. Yet Britain is the norm, according to which that sense of 'community' is defined. The example may be a minor one, since the explanation for the omission is easily stated: staff at the Commonwealth Institute have long wanted a display devoted to Great Britain, but apparently HM Government have not yet willed the means. The omission here emphasises difference: it is the notion of difference between Britain, on the one hand (the unrepresented dominant; the known; the familiar; the metropolis; the constant; the yardstick of measurement) against all those others (the represented subordinate; the lesser-known; the exotic; the colony; the 'developing'; the therefore-to-be-constantly-evaluated) – but somehow never against each other, always against the norm of Britain, the metropolis.

The consequence is not only that we are made to see these others through a British focus, but at the same time it serves to iron out, erase, difference between the others themselves; we have consciously to concentrate upon thinking of (say) Canada, or Botswana, or Jamaica, or Australia, as having identities independent of their membership of the Commonwealth, since such a privileging marginalizes: as examples, take the French as well as the United States dimensions to Canadian society; the Southern African dimension to Botswana; the French and Spanish dimensions in the Caribbean; the Pacific contexts in Australia. In each case there is the endeavour to retain for the 'Mother Country' a centripetal force and focus in the face of recent real relations, which have invariably been centrifugal – away from the centre; towards difference, regionality, identity. Such a reading is explicitly denied by the third key proposition in the lecture, namely that the Commonwealth '. . . represents the supremacy of community over otherness'. Now, I have some considerable difficulty with these terms 'community' and 'otherness', especially in their recent popular usages, particularly in the mass media and in the caring professions and parastatal agencies. But the drift of the usages seems to be clear: they have become euphemisms to replace that relatively recent arrival, 'ethnic', which is, itself, a replacement for words like 'coon' or 'nigger' in the heyday of Empire, or 'cannibal' or 'savage' in the days of Europe's first encounters with its 'others'. But this popular usage cuts both ways. I cannot accept the description of myself as 'other', since to do so would be to cooperate in the denial of my identity; furthermore, are not those who seek to classify me in this way, to me, 'the other'? The history of colonial experience[6] reveals that claims about 'community' have usually had the effect of continuing to impose inferiority. Such an assertion may sound harsh, but let us examine some implications, since these are also important for the role of the questionmark, itself still to be interrogated.

Assume that we accept that 'community' is preferable to 'otherness', but that we bear in mind that the forms of rationality, as well as its norms, are specifically not those of the 'other'. What ensues then? Since there are clear and commonsense ways in which distinctions are made about the categories, then how, if I am excluded by my categorisation as an 'other', do I become part of the preferred 'community', since it is precisely because I am defined as 'other' that I can never be incorporated. Furthermore, since it is assumed that my overriding wish is to be part of this 'community', I am left in a neat double bind: to question such an assumption is to demonstrate the extent to which I need to be incorporated; to express my admiration for it is to demonstrate the extent to which I will forever fall short. Whether I win gold medals (Daley Thompson) or acquire some element, seen as quintessentially 'British' (Rupert Murdoch) or write acclaimed works of the imagination (e.g. that new category, the 'black British' writer), there is something which, by the norms discussed above, will always be prevent me from ever being quite pukka. How the Commonwealth represents the triumph of 'community' is then difficult to see, particularly since the additional consequence of the assertion will be to gloss over difference, not now between member states, but within them: it is the English-speaking Raj that is privileged, or Briton over Boer or Bantu. Events in (say) Grenada, or Sri Lanka, or the Nigerian Civil War, can be explained in terms of the failure to apply, in these places, that mode of statecraft which expresses the British 'genius', and out of which emanates the concept of 'community': the 'Westminster model'.

If the case for 'community' can be sustained at all, it must be based in the experiences of the everyday lives of the people who inhabit the many spaces which constitute the Commonwealth. These experiences are usually represented by the artifacts which give expression to those experiences; they include literature, music, the visual arts, dance, etc. Yet not once in the lecture is reference made to this vast body of work by writers and artists from the Commonwealth – including the U.K. – so that we are confronted with a double exclusion: firstly, implicitly contained within the exclusion, there appears to be a general theory that it is possible to discuss notions of 'community' without reference to the cultural forms through which these are expressed; secondly, and in consequence, the elimination of the need to evaluate the artifacts themselves. Even the most cursory and superficial examination will reveal that, although it can be argued that the technical forms as well as the general spirit of these productions clearly have their origins in the historic links with Britain, these are regionally and culturally specific: whether it is the painting of Sidney Nolan in Australia or that of Cazabon in Trinidad; the novels of Wilson Harris in Guyana or Morley Callaghan in Canada; the poetry of Allen Curnow in New Zealand or Taban lo Liyong in Uganda; the drama of Soyinka in Nigeria or David Williamson in Australia, these artifacts demonstrate the search for a local habitation and a name. And it is precisely because of that fidelity to specificity, the rejection of the alien and imposed metropolitan ethic, that this is not simply a regional or 'provincial' art, but one that transcends such restrictive bounds.

The position may be put in the form of a question: if the Commonwealth represents the supremacy of community over otherness, where is the calypso that celebrates that assertion? or the dance? or the film? or the play? The reverse seems to be true: the artifacts chart the growth of feelings of alienation from whatever remnants of belief in such a sense of community might have existed, especially in the aftermath of the postwar period of emigration 'home' after the end of the Second World War (Sam Selvon, George Lamming) as well as of those born here, or who have lived here for most of their lives (Linton Kwesi Johnson; Grace Nichols; Caryl Phillips). It is these islands which, for creative artists from the Commonwealth, have become the 'other'.

How, then, do we evaluate Professor Ramphal's lecture, especially with reference to its timeliness? For all its optimism about the achievements of the Commonwealth, the lecture is couched in curiously pessimistic language. The exhortations to 'keep the faith' recall another great set-piece peroration. When, in *Troilus and Cressida* (Act I, Scene iii) Ulysses reflects upon the effect of the abrogation of order and degree to the Greek princes who are his audience on the stage, it can be assumed that his real audience in the theatre of the time would have been aware that the statement regarding hierarchical communal and international relations was not a statement about what actually existed, or about what had ever existed (except as an ideal), but rather about the gap between form and substance. Some members of that real audience and perhaps even some members of the audience on stage (Nestor? Achilles?) were aware, additionally, that the speech could be interpreted as an attempt to impose order upon elements of an increasingly recalcitrant populace, which had broken free of some of the outmoded forms and ideas about which Ulysses was lecturing. If, to pursue the analogy, Professor

Ramphal is cast in the role of a latter-day Ulysses, and the guests at the lecture are the princes on stage, then where is the absent auditorium, and who are the paying audience? We are presented here, with the final omission in the lecture and perhaps the most interesting one, since those absentees are the counterparts of that real seventeenth-century audience, independent interpreters of the events enacted in front of them. Given an opportunity to be present, some of them, too, would be aware that the story of the supremacy of community over otherness, like the story of order and degree, cannot be sustained. It is not that they do not want to believe; they would dearly love to do so, but their exclusion forces them not only into seeking alternative myths, but also to distrust the stories they hear, second-hand, about the places from which they have been excluded.

It appears to me, therefore, that if the popular sense of Commonwealth as either a body racked by internal dissent based upon outdated notions of cultural dominance, or one that it is essentially ineffectual, gains credence, it will become increasingly irrelevant, except to those who immediately sustain it, or are sustained by it. For that to happen would be a pity. What seems incontestable is the need for it to survive – indeed, for it to grow. For that to happen the organisation will have to transform itself radically – in order to assert (paradoxically almost, it would appear) not a sense of 'community', but the richness of difference, of specificity, which will enable it to play a role on the stages of the world.

NOTES

1. C. B.Macpherson, *The Political Theory of Possessive Individualism: Hobbes to Locke.* Oxford: O.U.P. 1962; *Democratic Theory: Essays in Retrieval,* Oxford: Clarendon Press,1973. A. S. P. Woodhouse, *Puritanism and Liberty: Being the Army Debates (1647-49),* London: Everyman (1974), 1986; C. Hill, *Milton and the English Revolution,* London: Faber,1977; *Some Intellectual Consequences of the English Revolution,* London: Weidenfeld, 1980.
2. See e.g. Paul Gilroy, *There Ain't No Black in the Union Jack: The Cultural Politics of Race and Nation,* London: Hutchinson, 1987.
3. I use inverted commas throughout to refer to the white minority regime and to constructions which privilege that society.
4. Recent studies include Herbert Adam, *Ethnic Power Mobilized,* New Haven: Yale U.P.1979; T. Dunbar Moodie, *The Rise of Afrikanerdom,* Berkeley, University of California Press, 1975; Andre du Toit & Hermann Giliomee, *Afrikaner Political Thought,* Cape Town: David Philip, 1983.
5. The recent initiative to found a 'Commonwealth University' is encouraging; the technical expertise of The Open University will, clearly, be of considerable importance.

It will, however, be interesting to see how some of the ideological issues implications – which will have immense pedagogical implications – will be resolved.

6. Peter Hulme, *Colonial Encounters: Europe and the Native Caribbean 1492-1797*, London: Methuen, 1986.

9: HILARY PERRATON
The Commonwealth of Learning

There is a particular reason why the invitation from the editors to contribute a progress report on the Commonwealth of Learning to this anthology of Commonwealth cultural explorations could not have been more appropriate.[1] It was at Exeter that the inquiry into Commonwealth co-operation in distance education and open learning, which was to result in the Commonwealth of Learning, was first revealed. That revelation had not been entirely foreseen. However, Professor Ramphal decided to build upon the happy coincidence of the occasion of his public lecture at the University and the impending announcement of his appointment of a Commonwealth Expert Group on Distance Education chaired by Professor Asa Briggs, Lord Briggs of Lewes, to inform members of the University and the local media about what was afoot. In a real sense, therefore, the Centre for American and Commonwealth Arts and Studies of Exeter University had a part in the launching of the plans for the Commonwealth of Learning. This note on progress will, I hope, show how far those plans have advanced in the 18 months or so since then.

It is the firm expectation of the 48 Commonwealth member countries, acting through the Commonwealth Secretariat, that the Commonwealth of Learning, an entirely new Agency to promote co-operation in distance education, will very shortly be set up. The plans for the new Agency were approved in principle by Commonwealth Heads of Government at their meeting in Vancouver in late 1987. In the first half of 1988, a working group chaired by Dr John Daniel, President of Laurentian University of Sudbury in Canada and an international authority on distance education, looked at ways and means of promoting Commonwealth co-operation along lines sketched out by the Briggs Report, *Towards a Commonwealth of Learning*. As a result of the work of these two groups, and of the political backing received from Commonwealth countries, it is hoped that by the end of 1988 the legal steps will be taken to create the new Agency, its governing board will meet and its first staff members will be appointed.

The proposals for the Commonwealth of Learning weave together a number of strands of social and intellectual history. One strand is that of Commonwealth co-operation in education. This predates the establishment of the Commonwealth itself, as the Association of Commonwealth Universities has just celebrated 75 years of co-operative activity. Shared educational assumptions, along with the common law and the use of the English language, are among the strongest links between the countries of the Commonwealth, and must greatly reinforce the thesis of a common Commonwealth culture; our colleges and universities have been enriched by the international movement of students and staff.

But – and this weaves in another of the threads – student mobility has itself been stretched and weakened by economic and political forces over the last ten years: with the downturn in the world economy and with higher fees for overseas students it has become more difficult for them to move from one country to another. This in turn led the Commonwealth Standing Committee on Student Mobility, set up in 1982 specifically to monitor the situation, to ask how far distance education might make possible a new kind of sharing of educational resources. That idea went on to the agenda of the Commonwealth Heads of Government meeting in 1985 who were, in the words of their Communique, 'particularly encouraged by the potential for collaboration in higher education through distance education and the use of new technologies'. They asked the Secretary-General to 'explore the scope for new Commonwealth initiatives in the field of open learning'.

Two other threads link demand and supply. Demand for education in the Third World far outstrips what hard pressed governments can afford to supply. It does so most dramatically and dangerously where, as in parts of Africa, the state of world trade and finance has made countries poorer rather than richer over the last decade. But at the same time the development of communications technology presents us with opportunities. As the Briggs Report says:

> In much of the developing Commonwealth educational resources are constrained just when more people than ever before want access tolearning and could benefit from it. In many places opportunities have been reduced and the quality of education has been eroded. The gates to student mobility have narrowed.

> This is, however, a time of convergence between the worldwide need to extend and develop educational opportunities and the worldwide

expansion of communication channels through which such needs can be met. The techniques of distance education make it possible for Commonwealth education to seize the opportunities presented by this convergence.[2]

To seize these opportunities, the Briggs group saw that it was necessary to create a new institution. This view commended itself both to Commonwealth education ministers, meeting in Nairobi in July 1987, and to Heads of Government subsequently, when they 'agreed to create a Commonwealth institution to promote co-operation in distance education, which may become the University of the Commonwealth for co-operation in distance education'.

One major area of action will be the exchange and development of teaching materials. There have already been small beginnings in co-operation on the use of materials and on their development between institutions within the Commonwealth. But this has been on a scale quite out of proportion with the long-term needs, partly because of the lack of any agency devoted to promoting activities of this kind. The Briggs group declared boldly:

> Our long-term aim is that any learner, anywhere in the Common-wealth, shall be able to study any distance-teaching programme available from any bona fide college or university in the Common-wealth. The new institution would seek to achieve this working in a co-operative partnership with existing colleges, universities and other institutions of post-secondary education.[3]

That is a long way off. In the first year or so, the Commonwealth of Learning is likely to promote a small number of exchanges and pro-grammes of co-operative development and teaching materials. When the governing board is established it will determine the areas in which this work is to start. But one thing is clear: the use of teaching materials may be as important as a way of supporting the internal teaching of universities and colleges as it is for reaching external students. In a Commonwealth where more than half the member countries have a population of less than 5 million, the capacity of distance education to bring resources that enrich and broaden the curriculum in small educational institutions is of central importance to educational expansion.

Secondly, the Commonwealth of Learning will engage in a variety of activities which will promote the institutional development of distance teaching colleges and universities. Both the Briggs group and the Daniel group saw that there was work to be done in the exchange of information, in training, in using communication technology to link institutions, and in research and evaluation. Again, detailed programmes will be drawn up by the governing board once it is established. As with the exchange of materials, it is the intention to work closely with existing agencies and to complement and support their work not, to compete with or duplicate it.

The Commonwealth of Learning's third group of activities has to do with support for individual students. Here it is important to stress one negative point: it is not the intention that the Commonwealth of Learning should itself enroll individual students throughout the Commonwealth. It would be unrealistic to have a new institution located in any one part of the Commonwealth attempting to enroll students Commonwealth-wide and provide support to them. Rather, the real need is to support the work of individual institutions which, country by country, are already in touch with their students and potential students. Support for individual students is expected to take two forms. In some cases there may be scope for consultancy or assistance to help with the establishment of local teaching and support services. More generally, there is a problem which lies at the heart of Commonwealth co-operation and exchange: if students in one country are using materials prepared in another, they need to be assured that they can get credit for the work they do with them. The Commonwealth of Learning will address the problems of credit transfer particularly as these apply to distance education; as part of the planning activities for the new Agency, the British Government is funding a study of this issue in more depth.

The Commonwealth of Learning will have its headquarters in Vancouver where the Government of British Columbia has made office accommodation available in the centre of the city. But the staff will not be huge or highly centralised: possibly 20 in post by the end of the first year of activity and perhaps double that number after four or five years. Much more activity will go on in the institutions with which the Commonwealth of Learning is co-operating. In some cases, too, activities will be undertaken on a regional basis. It is hoped to establish regional units to promote co-operation in distance education in various parts of the Commonwealth. In the Caribbean and the South Pacific, regional activities are already being undertaken by the two regional universities and their experience will be valuable. Offers to establish regional units in India and Nigeria have been welcomed. A proposal to base a small unit in Malta, with a particular interest in the educational problems of small states, will be considered by the governing board at its first meeting. Work on the exchange of information will be also based away from Vancouver. As the International Centre for Distance Learning, set up by the United Nations University with the Open University in Britain, already exists as an information centre at Milton Keynes, it makes more sense to build on that than to duplicate it.

The Commonwealth of Learning will need adequately to represent the interests of education and its students throughout the Commonwealth. To make this possible, Dr Daniel's working group recommended that a governing board should have overall responsibility for all its policy and activities. The group emphasised:

> the need for [the board] to be representative of all parts of the Commonwealth, including donor countries, to have members who can bring a knowledge of education generally including some with a specialist knowledge of distance education and members from the business and communication sectors. . .
>
> The board will require a balance between donors and others and between large countries and small. It will be necessary to ensure that it meets the needs of the Commonwealth as a whole and can act in the interests of Commonwealth developing countries, bearing in mind that any Commonwealth country should be able to benefit from the work of the Commonwealth of Learning.[4]

An appropriate structure has been worked out which takes these considerations into full account.

Initial finance for the Commonwealth of Learning is coming from governments. Some 15 million has been pledged for the first five years, by a range of Commonwealth governments, large and small. It is symbolically appropriate that, among the five largest donors, are India and Nigeria along with Britain, Brunei and Canada: in its finances, as in its government and its working, the Commonwealth of Learning represents and will represent both developing and industrialized nations. In due course it is expected that funds will be received on a project basis from a variety of sources, probably including industry and commerce as well as donor agencies and foundations.

The report of the working group chaired by Dr Daniel has been sent to governments for their consideration. It includes a draft Memorandum of Understanding which is the formal document that needs to be agreed by Commonwealth governments in order to establish the new Agency. It is hoped that it will prove possible for the Memorandum of Understanding to be agreed and for the governing board to be established in time for its first meeting to be held in Vancouver well before the end of 1988. In the meantime, the Commonwealth Secretariat is actively recruiting the first staff for the new Agency, starting with the post of president and some senior professional and administrative posts in the hope that the governing board will swiftly be able to make these appointments.

The time is right for this new venture. In the mid 1960s the time was right for the new developments in distance education that have reshaped our world. In Britain, the National Extension College and other institutions were working out how to link correspondence and broadcasting and so remold distance education. In the developing world distance education was being seized by newly independent countries not as a tool for reaching odd minorities of students but for centrally important educational jobs. Parallel paths to the British one were being taken in the United States and France. All those involved were, within national boundaries and similar ways, responding to demands for the expansion of education and to opportunities presented by a new awareness of what distance education might be.

Today there is a new and shared perception of international need and international opportunity. The creation of the Commonwealth of Learning, and European Association of Open Universities, the *Centre International Francophone de Formation à Distance* and the International Technological University are giving institutional form to these perceptions. In that earlier period of experiment and excitement it was observed that distance teaching marked the industrialisation of education. Today it can be seen that the techniques of distance education are, like more conventional industry, no respecter of frontiers. The expansion of international co-operation in this field may be as much a feature of the early 90s as expansion of distance education itself was in the late 60s and early 70s.

Although the word 'open' does not appear in the title of the new Agency, the Commonwealth of Learning is an open institution and at a very open stage in its development. It is open to new ideas and requests from all Commonwealth countries. It is open to perceptions of the educational needs to which it should respond. It is open to shaping forces as only a genuinely new institution can be.

NOTES

1. This Afterword has been adapted for this volume from a paper delivered to the Conference of the International Council for Distance Education at Oslo in August 1988. Dr. Perraton writes in a personal capacity and his views do not necessarily represent those of the Commonwealth Secretariat.

2. Commonwealth Secretariat, *Towards a Commonwealth of Learning* (The Briggs Report), London: Commonwealth Secretariat, 1987, paras. 4-5.

3. *ibid,* para 156.

4. Commonwealth Secretariat, *The Commonwealth of Learning: Institutional Arrangements for Commonwealth Co-operation in Distance Education*, London: Commonwealth Secretariat, 1988, paras. 29-30.

Notes on Contributors

Maria Couto, who has a doctorate from the Jawaharlal Nehru University, New Delhi, has lectured at Dhenge College of Bombay and Lady Shzi Ram College, University of Delhi. She has recently published *Graham Greene: On the Frontier: Politics and Religion in the Novels.* Currently based in London, she is working on an edition of Conrad's *Heart of Darkness.*

David Lowenthal is Emeritus Professor of Geography at University College London. He has worked extensively in the Commonwealth Caribbean and has done research in Australia and New Zealand. He is particularly interested in island societies and environments. His books include *The Past is a Foreign Country* and *West Indian Societies.*

John MacKenzie is Senior Lecturer in History at the University of Lancaster. He is the author of *Propaganda and Empire, The Empire of Nature: Hunting, Conservation and British Imperialism,* editor of *Imperialism and Popular Culture,* and General Editor of the Manchester University Press series 'Studies in Imperialism'. He is currently working on studies of conservation in the Commonwealth, imperialism and natural science, and late-nineteenth-century orientalism.

Richard Maltby lectures in film at the University of Exeter, and chairs American and Commonwealth Arts there. He has written and edited books on the American film industry, censorship and popular culture. He is General Editor of the 'Studies in American and Commonwealth Arts' series, published by the University of Exeter.

Alastair Niven is Director of Literature at the Arts Council of Great Britain. He has lectured on English and Commonwealth literatures at the Universities of Ghana, Leeds, Stirling, Aarhus and London. He edits the *Journal of Commonwealth Literature* and is Secretary of the Association for Commonwealth Literature and Language Studies. His writing includes studies of Elechi Amadi, Mulk Raj Anand, R.K.

Narayan and Raja Rao. He has also edited *Under Another Sky: the Commonwealth Poetry Prize Anthology*. He is a member of the International Advisory Panel for AmCAS.

Peter Quartermaine is Associate Director of AmCAS, and teaches American and Commonwealth Arts at the University of Exeter. He has written and edited books on Commonwealth literature and the visual arts. He serves on the Committee of the Sir Robert Menzies Centre for Australian Studies, London, and is a Fellow of the Royal Society of Arts.

Kenneth Parker is Professor of English and Cultural Studies in the North East London Polytechnic; he was born in South Africa, where his *The South African Novel in English: Essays in Criticism and Society* is banned. His most recent publication is an edition of *Dorothy Osborne: Letters to Sir William Temple, 1652-54*. He is a member of the International Advisory Panel for AmCAS.

Hilary Perraton is Chief Project Officer in the Education Programme of the Commonwealth Secretariat, with special responsibility for distance education. Before joining the Secretariat in 1984, he was co-director of Britain's International Extension College and from 1971 to 1984 acted widely as consultant on distance education in Africa. Dr Perraton is a former Director of Botswana Extension College.

Bernard Porter is Reader in History at the University of Hull. He divides his academic interests between modern imperialism and the history of the British domestic secret service. His books include *The Lion's Share: A Short History of British Imperialism 1850-1983* and *The Origins of the Vigilant State: The London Metropolitan Police Special Branch before the First World War*.

Sir Shridath S. Ramphal, who in 1986 was the first holder of the title Distinguished Visiting Professor at the University of Exeter, has been Commonwealth Secretary-General since 1975. He is the second to hold the office, and the first from the Third World. He was formerly Foreign Minister and Minister of Justice of his country, Guyana. He was a leading member of the 'Brandt' Independent Commission on International Development Issues, the 'Palme' Independent Commission on Disarmament and Security Issues and the 'Bruntland' World Commission on Environment and Development. In July 1987 he joined the newly-formed South Commission. From 1984-86 he was Chairman of the UN Commission on Development Planning. His many academic and professional honours have included, in 1988, the Chancellorship of the University of Guyana and the Albert Medal of the Royal Society of Arts awarded for his 'outstanding contributions towards accord within the Commonwealth and his promotion of the worldwide concept of our inseparable humanity'.

Michael Thorpe is Professor and Head of the English Department Mount Allison University, New Brunswick, Canada. He teaches Commonwealth literature and has published widely in the field, including studies of Doris Lessing and V.S. Naipaul, essays and poems in numerous journals; his most recent book is *The Observing Eye: Poems of the Third World*. He was Visiting Research Fellow at AmCAS in 1986-7.

Index